# 145 VEGETARIAN PASTA RECIPES

# 145 VEGETARIAN PASTA RECIPES

DELICIOUS PASTA AND NOODLE DISHES
FOR THE DISCERNING VEGETARIAN
COOK, SHOWN STEP BY STEP IN MORE
THAN 200 STUNNING PHOTOGRAPHS

VALERIE FERGUSON

southwater

This edition is published by Southwater, an imprint of Anness Publishing Ltd, Hermes House, 88–89 Blackfriars Road, London SE1 8HA; tel. 020 7401 2077; fax 020 7633 9499

www.southwaterbooks.com; www.annesspublishing.com

If you like the images in this book and would like to investigate using them for publishing, promotions or advertising, please visit our website www.practicalpictures.com for more information.

UK distributor: Book Trade Services; tel. 0116 2759086; fax 0116 2759090; uksales@booktradeservices.com; exportsales@booktradeservices.com
North American distributor: National Book Network; tel. 301 459 3366; fax 301 429 5746; www.nbnbooks.com
Australian distributor: Pan Macmillan Australia; tel. 1300 135 113; fax 1300 135 103; customer.service@macmillan.com.au
New Zealand distributor: David Bateman Ltd; tel. (09) 415 7664; fax (09) 415 8892

Publisher: Joanna Lorenz
Editor: Valerie Ferguson
Recipes by: Catherine Atkinson, Alex Barker, Michelle Berriedale-Johnson, Angela Boggiano, Janet Brinkworth, Carla Capalbo, Kit Chan, Jacqueline Clark, Maxine Clarke, Frances Cleary, Trish Davies, Roz Denny, Patrizia Diemling, Matthew Drennan, Sarah Edmonds, Rafi Fernandez, Christine France, Sarah Gates, Shirley Gill, Nicola Graimes, Rosamund Grant, Rebekah Hassan, Deh-Ta Hsuing, Shehzad Husain, Christine Ingram, Judy Jackson, Masaki Ko, Lesley Mackley, Norma MacMillan, Sue Maggs, Kathy Man, Elizabeth Martin, Sallie Morris, Annie Nichols, Maggie Pannell, Katherine Richmond, Anne Sheasby, Jenny Stacey, Liz Trigg, Hilaire Walden, Laura Washburn, Steven Wheeler, Judy Williams and Jeni Wright
Photographers: William Adams-Lingwood, Karl Adamson, Edward Allwright, David Armstrong, Steve Baxter, Nicki Dowey, James Duncan, John Freeman, Ian Garlick, Michelle Garrett, John Heseltine, Amanda Heywood, Janine Hosegood, David Jordan, Don Last, Patrick McLeavey, Thomas Odulate, Juliet Piddington and Peter Reilly
Designer: Carole Perks
Typesetter: Diane Pullen
Editorial Reader: Richard McGinlay
Production Controller: Claire Rae

## ETHICAL TRADING POLICY

## NOTES
Bracketed terms are intended for American readers.
For all recipes, quantities are given in both metric and imperial measures and, where appropriate, in standard cups and spoons. Follow one set of measures, but not a mixture, because they are not interchangeable.
Standard spoon and cup measures are level. 1 tsp = 5ml, 1 tbsp = 15ml, 1 cup = 250ml/8fl oz.
Australian standard tablespoons are 20ml. Australian readers should use 3 tsp in place of 1 tbsp for measuring small quantities.
American pints are 16fl oz/2 cups. American readers should use 20fl oz/2.5 cups in place of 1 pint when measuring liquids.
Electric oven temperatures in this book are for conventional ovens. When using a fan oven, the temperature will probably need to be reduced by about 10–20°C/20–40°F. Since ovens vary, you should check with your manufacturer's instruction book for guidance.
Medium (US large) eggs are used unless otherwise stated.
Main front cover image shows Pasta with Mixed Vegetable Medley – for recipe, see page 54.

## PUBLISHER'S NOTE

# Contents

Introduction 6

Soups & Salads 8

Quick & Easy Pasta 22

Pasta with Cheese & Nuts 36

Simply Vegetables 52

Special Occasions 70

Types of Pasta 88

Types of Noodle 91

Techniques 92

Index 94

# Introduction

No kitchen is properly stocked without a supply of pasta. Immensely versatile, it goes with a vast range of other ingredients, from mushrooms to cheese and from tomatoes to beans, to create a filling family supper in a matter of minutes or an elegant and sophisticated dish to

grace a dinner-party table. Popular with children and adults alike, it is inexpensive, convenient and a good source of protein, vitamins and minerals, as well as supplying sustained, slow-release energy. Best of all, it forms the basis of a repertoire of sensational vegetarian dishes, whether flavoursome soups, tempting appetizers, light lunches, midweek meals, refreshing salads or celebration suppers.

With more than 140 recipes, this book is packed with clever ideas to inspire even the most reluctant cook and features both Western pasta dishes and Asian noodles. Five chapters offer a comprehensive choice of classic dishes and traditional ways with pasta, as well as innovative and contemporary combinations that accord well with modern health guidelines. Soups & Salads ranges from family favourites, such as Genoese Minestrone, to the exotic Burmese noodle salad, Thamin Lethok. Quick & Easy Pasta is the place to start for those with a busy lifestyle and little time to spend in the kitchen. In the time it takes for the pasta to cook – about ten minutes –

you can conjure up a magical sauce from tender vegetables, creamy cheese, fresh herbs and even courgette (zucchini) flowers to produce a virtually instant meal. Pasta with Cheese & Nuts rings the changes on this classic combination. Forget boring macaroni cheese – try, instead, Macaroni Cheese Pie, a delicately spiced Caribbean variation, bursting with tomatoes, onions and sweetcorn, or indulge yourself with

the wonderfully rich and creamy Paglia e Fieno with Walnuts & Gorgonzola. Simply Vegetables is just that – every imaginable combination of pasta with beans, tomatoes, (bell) peppers, broccoli, mushrooms, courgettes (zucchini), peas, sweetcorn and even cabbage. From fresh-tasting Mediterranean vegetable medleys to fragrantly spiced Chinese mushrooms, there is sure to be something that will delight. Special Occasions

features a spectacular collection of exquisite pasta dishes. You can choose easy entertaining with the elegant simplicity of Tagliatelle with Chanterelles or show off your culinary expertise with the magnificent Coriander Ravioli with Pumpkin Filling. Whether a family gathering, a casual lunch with friends or a formal dinner party, pasta is perfect and sure to impress.

Finally, the book features an invaluable reference section, beginning with a useful illustrated guide to some of the many different types of pasta and noodles so that you can experiment with a variety of shapes and flavours. This is followed by step-by-step instructions for making pasta at home. While this is time-consuming and may be a little tricky at first, it is immensely satisfying, great fun and unutterably delicious. Try different flavours, such as tomato or spinach, and don't worry if you don't have a pasta machine, there are easy-to-follow instructions for

cutting a variety of pasta shapes by hand. A simple guide to cooking times will ensure that your pasta dishes are always what Italians call *al dente* – which could fairly be translated as toothsome or with bite.

Fresh or dried, home-made or from a packet, long ribbons or curly shapes, pasta is the perfect vegetarian ingredient for every occasion and all seasons of the year.

# SOUPS & SALADS

Pasta and noodles give soups substance and "bite", as well as looking very attractive. There is a huge range of tiny shapes designed for just this purpose and you can match both size and shape to the other ingredients for a stunning effect. Pasta is traditionally paired with beans in Italian soups and this chapter includes classics, such as minestrone, as well as some rather more unusual dishes – whether a delicate broth to serve as an appetizer or a hearty one-pot meal. It also features a light vegetable stock that is not only useful as a basis for soups, but can also add flavour to many other vegetarian dishes. Whether partnered with vegetables, herbs, cheese or nuts, pasta makes wonderful – and sometimes very substantial – salads. They can be served as an appetizer, an accompaniment or even as a main course. There is a mouthwatering collection of Mediterranean recipes, packed with sun-ripened vegetables, that look just as delicious as they taste. Asian noodle salads are not, perhaps, so well known in the West as hot dishes, but they have a long and honourable tradition, especially in Thailand and Burma. Typically, they are beautifully presented and tossed with a subtle and piquant dressing – often with just a hint of hot spice. Summer or winter, main course or accompaniment and whatever your favourite flavour, you are sure to find just the right pasta salad.

# Classic Vegetarian Minestrone

You don't need meat to make a magnificent minestrone. This home-made version is a revelation based on pasta, beans and fresh vegetables.

**Serves 4**
45ml/3 tbsp olive oil
1 large leek, thinly sliced
2 carrots, chopped
1 courgette (zucchini), thinly sliced
115g/4oz whole green
   beans, halved
2 celery sticks, thinly sliced

1.5 litres/2½ pints/6 cups
   Vegetable Stock or water
400g/14oz can
   chopped tomatoes
15ml/1 tbsp fresh basil, chopped
5ml/1 tsp fresh thyme leaves,
   chopped, or 2.5ml/½ tsp
   dried thyme
400g/14oz can cannellini or
   kidney beans
50g/2oz/½ cup small pasta
   shapes or macaroni
freshly grated Parmesan cheese
   and chopped fresh parsley, to
   garnish (optional)

**1** Heat the oil in a large pan, add the leek, carrots, courgette, green beans and celery and mix well. Heat until sizzling, then cover, lower the heat and sweat the vegetables for 15 minutes, shaking the pan occasionally.

**2** Add the stock or water, tomatoes and herbs and season with salt and pepper to taste. Bring to the boil, replace the lid and simmer gently for about 30 minutes.

**3** Add the beans, with the can juices, then tip in the pasta. Simmer until the pasta is *al dente*. Check the seasoning and adjust if necessary.

**4** Serve in warmed bowls, sprinkled with the grated Parmesan cheese and parsley, if you like.

**Cook's Tip**
*The flavour of minestrone improves if it is made a day or two ahead and stored in the refrigerator. It can also be frozen and then gently reheated.*

# Genoese Minestrone

Packed with vegetables, this soup has a good strong flavour, making it an excellent vegetarian dish.

**Serves 4–6**
45ml/3 tbsp olive oil
1 onion, finely chopped
2 celery sticks, thinly sliced
1 large carrot, diced
150g/5oz green beans, cut into
   short lengths
1 courgette (zucchini), thinly sliced
1 potato, cut into 1cm/
   ½in cubes
¼ Savoy cabbage, shredded
1 small aubergine (eggplant), cut
   into 1cm/½in cubes

200g/7oz can cannellini beans,
   drained and rinsed
2 Italian plum tomatoes, chopped
1.2 litres/2 pints/5 cups
   Vegetable Stock
90g/3½ oz dried spaghetti
salt and freshly ground
   black pepper

**For the pesto**
about 20 fresh basil leaves
1 garlic clove
10ml/2 tsp pine nuts
15ml/1 tbsp freshly grated
   Parmesan cheese
15ml/1 tbsp freshly grated
   Pecorino cheese
30ml/2 tbsp olive oil

**1** Heat the oil in a large pan, add the onion, celery and carrot and cook over a low heat, stirring frequently, for about 5–7 minutes, until the onion is soft and translucent.

**2** Tip in the green beans, courgette, potato and cabbage. Stir-fry over a medium heat for about 3 minutes. Add the aubergine, cannellini beans and tomatoes, and stir-fry for 2–3 minutes more. Pour in the stock with salt and pepper to taste. Bring to the boil. Stir well, cover and lower the heat. Simmer for 40 minutes, stirring occasionally.

**3** Meanwhile, make the pesto. Process all the ingredients in a food processor until the mixture forms a smooth sauce, adding 15–45ml/1–3 tbsp water through the feeder tube, if necessary.

**4** Break the pasta into small pieces and add it to the soup. Simmer, stirring frequently, for 5 minutes. Gently stir in the pesto, then simmer until the pasta is *al dente*. Taste for seasoning. Serve hot, in warmed soup plates or bowls.

# Cauliflower Soup with Farfalle

Serve this smooth, mildly cheese-flavoured soup with Melba toast for an elegant dinner-party appetizer.

**Serves 6**
1 large cauliflower
1.2 litres/2 pints/5 cups
    Vegetable Stock
175g/6oz/1½ cups dried farfalle
150ml/ ¼ pint/ ⅔ cup single
    (light) cream or milk
freshly grated nutmeg
pinch of cayenne pepper
60ml/4 tbsp freshly grated
    Parmesan cheese
salt and freshly ground
    black pepper

**1** Divide the cauliflower into florets. Bring the stock to the boil and add the florets. Simmer for 10 minutes, or until tender. Transfer the florets with a slotted spoon to a food processor.

**2** Add the pasta to the pan and simmer until *al dente*. Drain, reserve the pasta, and pour the liquid into the food processor.

**3** Add the cream or milk, nutmeg and cayenne, process until smooth, then press through a sieve into the clean pan. Stir in the cooked pasta. Reheat the soup and stir in the Parmesan. Taste and adjust the seasoning, then serve.

# Melba Toast

Crisp Melba toast is wonderful with all types of soup.

3–4 thin slices day-old
    white bread
freshly grated Parmesan cheese,
    for sprinkling
1.5ml/ ¼ tsp paprika

**1** Toast the bread on both sides. Cut off the crusts and split each slice in half horizontally.

**2** Scrape off any doughy bits and sprinkle with the Parmesan and paprika.
**3** Place cut side up on a baking sheet under a medium grill (broiler) until the toast is golden and has curled at the edges. Watch it closely as it burns easily.

# Beetroot & Ravioli Soup

Cook your own beetroot for this jewel-like soup.

**Serves 4–6**
1 quantity Basic Pasta Dough
egg white, beaten, for brushing
plain (all-purpose) flour,
    for dusting
1 small onion, finely chopped
2 garlic cloves, crushed
5ml/1 tsp fennel seeds
600ml/1 pint/2½ cups
    Vegetable Stock
225g/8oz cooked beetroot (beet)
30ml/2 tbsp fresh orange juice
dill leaves, to garnish

*For the filling*
115g/4oz/1¾ cups mushrooms,
    finely chopped
1 small onion, finely chopped
1–2 garlic cloves, crushed
5ml/1 tsp chopped fresh thyme
15ml/1 tbsp chopped
    fresh parsley
90ml/6 tbsp fresh white
    breadcrumbs
salt and freshly ground
    black pepper
large pinch of freshly
    grated nutmeg

**1** Process all the filling ingredients in a food processor or blender. Set aside.

**2** Roll the pasta into thin sheets. Lay one piece over a ravioli tray and put a teaspoonful of the filling into each depression. Brush around the edges of each ravioli with egg white. Cover with another sheet of pasta and press the edges together. Cut into squares. Transfer to a floured dishtowel and rest for 1 hour.

**3** Cook the ravioli, in batches, in a pan of boiling, salted water for 2 minutes. Lift out on a slotted spoon and drop into a bowl of cold water. Leave for 5 seconds. Drain and place on a tray.

**4** Put the onion, garlic and fennel seeds into a pan with 150ml/ ¼ pint/ ⅔ cup of the stock. Bring to the boil, lower the heat, cover and simmer for 5 minutes, until tender. Peel and finely dice the beetroot. Set aside 60ml/4 tbsp for the garnish. Add the rest to the soup with the remaining stock. Bring to the boil.

**5** Add the orange juice and ravioli and simmer until *al dente*. Serve, garnished with the reserved beetroot and dill leaves.

# Star-gazer Vegetable Soup

If you have time, it is worth making your own vegetable stock for this soup.

**Serves 4**
1 yellow (bell) pepper
2 large courgettes (zucchini)

2 large carrots
1 kohlrabi
900ml/1½ pints/3¾ cups well-
   flavoured Vegetable Stock
50g/2oz rice vermicelli
salt and freshly ground
   black pepper

**1** Cut the pepper into quarters, removing the seeds and core. Cut the courgettes and carrots lengthways into 5mm/¼in slices and slice the kohlrabi into 5mm/¼in rounds.

**2** Using tiny confectionery cutters, stamp out decorative shapes from the vegetables. Place in a pan, add the stock and bring to the boil. Lower the heat and simmer for 10 minutes. Season.

**3** Meanwhile, place the vermicelli in a heatproof bowl, cover with boiling water and set aside for 4 minutes. Drain, divide among four warmed soup bowls, ladle the hot soup over and serve.

# Vegetable Stock

This is a delicately flavoured stock, suitable for many clear broths and soups.

**Makes about 2.5 litres/
4 pints/10 cups**
2 onions, chopped
2 leeks, sliced
3 garlic cloves, crushed
2 carrots, chopped
4 celery sticks, sliced

a large strip of pared lemon rind
12 parsley stalks
a few fresh thyme sprigs
2 bay leaves
2.5 litres/4 pints/10 cups water

**1** Put the ingredients in a large pan. Bring to the boil. Skim the surface, lower the heat and simmer for 30 minutes.

**2** Strain the stock and leave to cool.

# Cheat's Shark's Fin Soup

Shark's fin soup is a renowned delicacy. In this poor man's vegetarian version, cellophane noodles, cut into short lengths, mimic shark's fin needles.

**Serves 4–6**
4 dried Chinese mushrooms
25ml/1½ tbsp dried wood ears
115g/4oz cellophane noodles
30ml/2 tbsp vegetable oil
2 carrots, cut into fine strips

114g/4oz canned bamboo
   shoots, rinsed, drained and cut
   into fine strips
1 litre/1¾ pints/4 cups
   Vegetable Stock
15ml/1 tbsp soy sauce
15ml/1 tbsp arrowroot, mixed to
   a paste with 30ml/2 tbsp water
5ml/1 tsp sesame oil
salt and freshly ground
   black pepper
2 spring onions (scallions), finely
   chopped, to garnish

**1** Soak the mushrooms and wood ears separately in warm water for 20 minutes. Drain well. Remove and discard the stems from the mushrooms and slice the caps thinly. Cut the wood ears into fine strips, discarding any hard pieces. Soak the noodles in hot water until soft. Drain and cut into short lengths. Set aside until required.

**2** Heat the oil in a large, heavy pan. Add the mushrooms and stir-fry over a medium heat for 2 minutes. Add the wood ears and stir-fry for 2 minutes, then stir in the carrots, bamboo shoots and noodles.

**3** Add the vegetable stock to the pan. Bring to the boil, lower the heat and simmer gently for 15–20 minutes. Season to taste with salt and pepper and stir in the soy sauce.

**4** Pour the arrowroot paste into the soup, stirring constantly to prevent the formation of lumps as the soup continues to simmer. Allow to thicken slightly.

**5** Remove the pan from the heat. Stir in the sesame oil, then pour the soup into warmed individual soup bowls. Sprinkle each portion with chopped spring onions to garnish, and serve immediately.

# Pasta Soup with Pulses

A simple, country-style soup. The shape of the pasta and the beans complement one another beautifully.

**Serves 4–6**
30ml/2 tbsp olive oil
1 onion, chopped
2 carrots, chopped
2 celery sticks, sliced
400g/14oz can chickpeas, rinsed and drained
200g/7oz can cannellini beans, rinsed and drained
150ml/ $^{1}/_{4}$ pint/ $^{2}/_{3}$ cup passata (bottled strained tomatoes)
120ml/4fl oz/ $^{1}/_{2}$ cup water
1.5 litres/2 $^{1}/_{2}$ pints/6 cups Vegetable Stock
2 fresh rosemary sprigs
200g/7oz/scant 2 cups dried conchiglie
salt and freshly ground black pepper
freshly grated Parmesan cheese, to serve

**1** Heat the oil in a large pan, add the fresh vegetables and cook over a low heat, stirring frequently, for 5–7 minutes.

**2** Stir in the chickpeas and cannellini beans. Cook for about 5 minutes, then stir in the passata and water. Continue to cook, stirring constantly, for 2–3 minutes.

**3** Add 475ml/16fl oz/2 cups of the stock, one of the rosemary sprigs and season with salt and pepper to taste. Bring to the boil, cover, then simmer gently, stirring occasionally, for 1 hour.

**4** Pour in the remaining stock and bring to the boil. Add the pasta. Lower the heat and simmer, stirring frequently, until the pasta is *al dente*.

**5** Taste for seasoning. Remove the rosemary sprig. Serve in warmed bowls, topped with Parmesan and rosemary leaves.

> **Variation**
> If you like, crush one to two garlic cloves and fry them with the vegetables in step 1.

# Calabrian Pasta & Bean Soup

In Southern Italy, this soup is called *millecose*, meaning "a thousand things" as it is based on whatever ingredients are to hand.

**Serves 4–6**
75g/3oz/scant $^{1}/_{2}$ cup brown lentils
475ml/16fl oz/2 cups cold water
15g/ $^{1}/_{2}$ oz dried mushrooms
175ml/6fl oz/ $^{3}/_{4}$ cup warm water
30ml/2 tbsp olive oil
$^{1}/_{2}$ red (bell) pepper, cored, seeded and diced
1 carrot, diced
1 celery stick, diced
2 shallots, finely chopped
1 garlic clove, finely chopped
$^{1}/_{2}$ fresh red chilli, seeded and chopped
a little chopped fresh flat leaf parsley
1.5 litres/2 $^{1}/_{2}$ pints/6 cups Vegetable Stock
150g/5oz/ $^{2}/_{3}$ cup each drained canned red kidney beans, cannellini beans and chickpeas, rinsed
115g/4oz/1 cup dried penne
salt and freshly ground black pepper
chopped flat leaf parsley, to garnish
freshly grated Pecorino cheese, to serve

**1** Put the lentils in a pan, pour in the cold water and bring to the boil. Lower the heat and simmer, stirring occasionally, for 15–20 minutes, until just tender. Meanwhile, soak the dried mushrooms in the measured warm water for 15–20 minutes.

**2** Drain the lentils and rinse under cold water. Drain the soaked mushrooms through kitchen paper and reserve the soaking liquid. Finely chop the mushrooms and set them aside.

**3** Heat the oil in a pan and fry the red pepper, carrot, celery, shallots, garlic and chilli over a low heat, stirring constantly, for 5–7 minutes. Add the parsley and stock, then the mushrooms with their soaking liquid. Bring to the boil, add the beans and chickpeas and season. Cover, and simmer for 20 minutes.

**4** Add the pasta and lentils. Bring the soup back to the boil, stirring. Simmer, stirring frequently, until the pasta is *al dente*. Season, then serve in warmed soup bowls, garnished with chopped parsley and with grated Pecorino.

# Thick Spinach & Pasta Soup

A complete meal in a bowl, this is a version of a classic Italian soup. Traditionally, the person who finds the bay leaf is honoured with a kiss from the cook.

**Serves 4**

75ml/5 tbsp olive oil
1 onion, chopped
½ celeriac, chopped
2 carrots, chopped
1 bay leaf
175ml/6fl oz/¾ cup white wine
1.2 litres/2 pints/5 cups
   Vegetable Stock
3 tomatoes, peeled and chopped
400g/14oz can borlotti beans,
   rinsed and drained
175g/6oz/1½ cups dried farfalle
250g/9oz spinach, washed and
   thick stalks removed
salt and freshly ground
   black pepper
50g/2oz/⅔ cup freshly grated
   Parmesan cheese, to serve

**1** Heat the olive oil in a large pan and add the onion, celeriac and carrots. Cook over a medium heat, stirring occasionally, for about 5 minutes, or until the vegetables are just beginning to soften.

**2** Add the bay leaf, wine, stock and tomatoes and bring to the boil. Lower the heat and simmer for 10 minutes, until the vegetables are just tender.

**3** Add the beans, bring the soup back to the boil, then stir in the pasta. Simmer, stirring occasionally, until the pasta is *al dente*.

**4** Season with salt and pepper to taste, add the spinach and cook for 2 minutes more. Serve in warmed bowls, sprinkled with the Parmesan.

> **Cook's Tip**
> *Avoid buying very large celeriac roots, as they tend to be woody. Peel carefully with a sharp knife to remove all traces of the brown, knobbly skin. Don't chop the flesh until you are ready to cook it, as it is apt to discolour. If necessary, place the chopped pieces in water acidulated with a little lemon juice.*

# Rustic Lentil & Pasta Soup

A thick wedge of fresh bread is all that's needed to turn this hearty soup into a warming meal.

**Serves 4–6**

175g/6oz/¾ cup brown lentils
3 garlic cloves
1 litre/1¾ pints/4 cups water
45ml/3 tbsp olive oil
25g/1oz/2 tbsp butter
1 onion, finely chopped
2 celery sticks, finely chopped
1.75 litres/3 pints/7 cups
   Vegetable Stock
pared rind and juice of 1 orange
a few fresh marjoram leaves
a few fresh basil leaves
leaves from 1 fresh thyme sprig
50g/2oz/½ cup dried tubetti
salt and freshly ground
   black pepper
tiny fresh herb leaves,
   to garnish

**1** Put the lentils in a large pan. Smash one garlic clove (there's no need to peel it first) and add it to the lentils. Pour in the measured water and bring to the boil. Lower the heat to a gentle simmer and cook, stirring occasionally, for 20 minutes, or until the lentils are just tender.

**2** Tip the lentils into a sieve, remove the garlic and set it aside. Rinse the lentils under cold water, then leave them to drain.

**3** Heat 30ml/2 tbsp of the oil with half the butter in a large pan. Add the onion and celery, and cook over a low heat, stirring frequently, for 5–7 minutes, until softened.

**4** Crush the remaining garlic, then peel and mash the reserved garlic. Add to the vegetables with the remaining oil and the lentils. Stir, then add the stock, orange juice, the fresh herbs and salt and pepper to taste. Bring to the boil, then simmer for 30 minutes, stirring occasionally.

**5** Cut the orange rind into thin strips, taking care to avoid including any of the bitter white pith. Add the pasta and orange rind strips to the soup and bring back to the boil, stirring constantly. Cook until the pasta is *al dente*. Stir in the remaining butter and taste for seasoning. Serve in warmed bowls, sprinkled with the herb leaves.

# Vegetable & Vermicelli Noodle Soup

With neatly shredded greens, thinly sliced mushrooms and fine noodles, this soup looks as good as it tastes.

**Serves 4**
1.2 litres/2 pints/5 cups
   Vegetable Stock
1 garlic clove, bruised
2.5cm/1in piece of fresh root
   ginger, cut into fine sticks
30ml/2 tbsp soy sauce
15ml/1 tbsp cider vinegar
75g/3oz/1 cup fresh shiitake or
   button (white) mushrooms,
   stalks removed and thinly sliced
2 large spring onions (scallions),
   thinly sliced on the diagonal
40g/1½ oz rice vermicelli or
   other fine noodles
175g/6oz Chinese leaves (Chinese
   cabbage), finely shredded
a few fresh coriander
   (cilantro) leaves

**1** Pour the stock into a pan. Add the garlic, ginger, soy sauce and vinegar. Bring to the boil, then cover and reduce the heat to very low. Simmer for 10 minutes. Remove the garlic clove.

**2** Add the mushrooms and spring onions and bring the soup back to the boil. Simmer for 5 minutes, stirring occasionally.

**3** Add the noodles and shredded Chinese leaves. Simmer for 3–4 minutes, or until the noodles and vegetables are just tender. Stir in the coriander leaves. Simmer for 1 minute more, then serve in warmed soup bowls.

**Cook's Tips**
• *To bruise the peeled garlic clove, crush it lightly with the blade of a cook's knife.*
• *To shred the Chinese leaves (Chinese cabbage), stack them six to eight at a time and roll up tightly parallel with the central rib. If the leaves are very large, roll them individually. With a very sharp knife, slice across the roll of leaves into fine shreds, guiding the side of the knife with the knuckles of the hand holding the roll. Be sure to cut straight down through the roll to avoid unattractive bruising on the leaves.*

# Japanese-style Noodle Soup

This delicate, fragrant soup is flavoured with the slightest hint of chilli.

**Serves 4**
1 litre/1¾ pints/4 cups water
45ml/3 tbsp mugi miso
200g/7oz udon noodles, soba
   noodles or Chinese egg noodles
30ml/2 tbsp sake or dry sherry
15ml/1 tbsp rice vinegar
45ml/3 tbsp Japanese soy sauce
115g/4oz asparagus tips or
   mangetouts (snow peas), thinly
   sliced on the diagonal
50g/2oz/scant 1 cup shiitake
   mushrooms, stalks removed and
   thinly sliced
1 carrot, sliced into
   fine strips
3 spring onions (scallions), thinly
   sliced on the diagonal
salt and freshly ground
   black pepper
5ml/1 tsp dried chilli flakes,
   to serve

**1** Bring the measured water to the boil in a pan. Put the miso in a heatproof bowl. Pour over 150ml/¼ pint/⅔ cup of the boiling water and stir until dissolved, then set aside.

**2** Meanwhile, cook the noodles in a separate pan of boiling water until just tender. Drain, rinse under cold water, then drain again. Set aside.

**3** Add the sake or sherry, vinegar and soy sauce to the pan of boiling water. Boil gently for 3 minutes, then lower the heat and stir in the miso mixture. Add the asparagus or mangetouts, mushrooms, carrot and spring onions. Simmer for 2 minutes or until the vegetables are just tender. Season to taste.

**4** Divide the noodles among four warmed bowls and pour the soup over. Serve immediately, sprinkled with the chilli flakes.

**Cook's Tip**
*Miso is made from fermented soya beans and is available as both a paste and a powder. There are several different varieties.*

# Chargrilled Pepper Salad

This is a good side salad to serve with dishes made from pulses or eggs.

**Serves 4**
1 large red (bell) pepper
1 large green (bell) pepper
250g/9oz/2¼ cups dried fusilli, preferably mixed colours
a handful of fresh basil leaves

a handful of fresh coriander (cilantro) leaves
1 garlic clove
salt and freshly ground black pepper

**For the dressing**
30ml/2 tbsp bottled pesto
juice of ½ lemon
60ml/4 tbsp extra virgin olive oil

**1** Preheat the grill (broiler). Cut the peppers in half and remove the cores and seeds. Place the peppers cut side down in a grill pan and grill (broil) for about 10 minutes, until the skin has blistered and charred. Put the hot peppers in a bowl, cover with several layers of kitchen paper and set aside until cool.

**2** Bring a large pan of lightly salted water to the boil and cook the pasta until it is *al dente*.

**3** Meanwhile, put the pesto, lemon juice and oil in a large bowl and whisk well to mix. Season to taste with salt and pepper.

**4** Drain the cooked pasta well and tip it into the bowl of dressing. Toss well to mix, then set aside to cool.

**5** When the peppers are cool enough to handle, peel them, then chop the flesh and add it to the pasta.

**6** Put the basil, coriander and garlic on a chopping board and chop them all together. Add to the pasta and toss to mix, then season to taste with salt and pepper and serve.

> **Cook's Tip**
> You can serve the salad at room temperature or chilled, whichever you like.

# Roasted Cherry Tomato & Rocket Salad

This is a good side salad to accompany vegetable kebabs which have been cooked on a barbecue. Roasted tomatoes are very juicy, with an intense, smoky-sweet flavour.

**Serves 4**
450g/1lb ripe baby Italian plum tomatoes, halved lengthways
75ml/5 tbsp extra virgin olive oil

2 garlic cloves, cut into thin slivers
225g/8oz/2 cups dried pipe
30ml/2 tbsp balsamic vinegar
2 pieces of sun-dried tomato in olive oil, drained and chopped
a large pinch of granulated sugar
1 handful of rocket (arugula), about 65g/2½oz
salt and freshly ground black pepper

**1** Preheat the oven to 190°C/375°F/Gas 5. Arrange the halved tomatoes cut side up in a roasting pan, drizzle 30ml/2 tbsp of the olive oil over them and sprinkle with the slivers of garlic. Season with salt and pepper to taste. Roast in the oven for 20 minutes, turning once.

**2** Meanwhile, bring a large pan of lightly salted water to the boil and cook the pasta until it is *al dente*.

**3** Put the remaining oil in a large bowl and add the vinegar, sun-dried tomatoes and sugar and season with a little salt and pepper to taste. Stir well to mix.

**4** Drain the pasta, add it to the bowl of dressing and toss to mix. Add the roasted tomatoes and mix gently.

**5** Just before serving, add the chopped rocket, toss lightly and adjust the seasoning, if necessary.

> **Variation**
> Add 150g/5oz diced mozzarella with the rocket (arugula).

# Avocado & Pasta Salad with Coriander

Served solo or as part of a selection of salads, this tasty combination is sure to please. The dressing is quite sharp, but very refreshing.

**Serves 4**
900ml/1½ pints/3¾ cups Vegetable Stock
115g/4oz/1 cup dried farfalle or conchiglie
4 celery sticks, finely chopped
2 avocados, peeled, stoned (pitted) and chopped
1 garlic clove, chopped
15ml/1 tbsp finely chopped fresh coriander (cilantro), plus some whole leaves to garnish
115g/4oz/1 cup grated mature (sharp) Cheddar cheese

*For the dressing*
150ml/¼ pint/⅔ cup extra virgin olive oil
15ml/1 tbsp cider vinegar
30ml/2 tbsp lemon juice
grated rind of 1 lemon
5ml/1 tsp Dijon mustard
15ml/1 tbsp roughly chopped fresh coriander (cilantro)
salt and freshly ground black pepper

**1** Pour the stock into a large pan. Bring to the boil and cook the pasta until *al dente*. Drain, rinse under cold water and drain again. Leave to cool.

**2** Mix the celery, avocados, garlic and chopped coriander in a bowl, and add the cooled pasta. Sprinkle with the grated Cheddar cheese.

**3** To make the dressing, put the oil, vinegar, lemon juice and rind, mustard and fresh coriander in a food processor and process until the coriander is finely chopped. Season to taste with salt and pepper. Serve the dressing separately or toss it with the salad. Serve, garnished with the coriander leaves.

# Avocado, Tomato & Mozzarella Pasta Salad

Dressed farfalle and sliced avocados make wonderful additions to a classic salad.

**Serves 4**
175g/6oz/1½ cups dried farfalle
6 ripe red tomatoes
225g/8oz mozzarella cheese
1 large ripe avocado
30ml/2 tbsp pine nuts, toasted
1 fresh basil sprig, to garnish

*For the dressing*
90ml/6 tbsp extra virgin olive oil
30ml/2 tbsp wine vinegar
5ml/1 tsp balsamic vinegar
5ml/1 tsp wholegrain mustard
pinch of sugar
30ml/2 tbsp chopped fresh basil
salt and freshly ground black pepper

**1** Bring a large pan of lightly salted water to the boil and cook the pasta until it is *al dente*. Drain, rinse under cold water, then drain again. Tip into a bowl and set aside to cool.

**2** Slice the tomatoes and mozzarella cheese into thin rounds. Cut the avocado in half, lift out the stone (pit) and peel off the skin. Slice the flesh lengthways.

**3** Arrange the tomato, mozzarella and avocado in overlapping slices around the edge of a flat serving plate.

**4** For the dressing, put the oil, wine vinegar, balsamic vinegar, mustard, sugar and basil into a small bowl and whisk until combined. Season to taste with salt and pepper.

**5** Add half the dressing to the pasta. Toss to coat, then pile into the centre of the plate. Pour over the remaining dressing, sprinkle over the pine nuts and garnish with the basil sprig. Serve immediately.

## Cook's Tip
*Choose tomatoes that are uniform in size.*

# Asparagus & Potato Pasta Salad with Parmesan

A meal in itself, this is a real treat when made with fresh asparagus just in season.

**Serves 4**
225g/8oz/2 cups wholewheat
   fusilli or spirali
60ml/4 tbsp extra virgin olive oil

350g/12oz baby new potatoes
225g/8oz fresh asparagus
115g/4oz piece of fresh
   Parmesan cheese, shaved
salt and freshly ground
   black pepper

**1** Bring a large pan of lightly salted water to the boil and cook the pasta until it is *al dente*. Drain, rinse briefly under cold water and drain again.

**2** Tip the pasta into a large bowl, add the olive oil, and season to taste with salt and pepper. Toss well and set aside.

**3** Put the potatoes in a pan of cold water. Bring to the boil and cook for 12–15 minutes, or until tender. Drain and toss with the pasta.

**4** Snap the woody ends off the asparagus. If the spears are very long, cut them in half. Blanch them in boiling salted water for 6 minutes until bright green and still crunchy. Drain. Plunge into cold water to stop them cooking, drain again and leave to cool. Dry on kitchen paper.

**5** Add the asparagus to the bowl and toss it with the potatoes and pasta. Season to taste, then transfer to a bowl. Garnish with a little Parmesan, and hand the rest around separately.

> **Cook's Tips**
> *Look out for Charlottes, which are among the most delicious salad potatoes. Rocket, Minerva and Colmo are all suitable varieties for this recipe.*

# Wholewheat Pasta Salad

This is easily assembled from any combination of seasonal vegetables.

**Serves 8**
2 medium carrots, chopped
175g/6oz/1½ cups fresh or
   thawed frozen peas
2 heads of broccoli, broken
   into florets
450g/1lb/4 cups dried
   wholewheat fusilli or penne
45ml/3 tbsp olive oil
1 red or yellow (bell) pepper
2 celery sticks
4 spring onions (scallions)

1 large tomato
75g/3oz/¾ cup pitted
   black olives, quartered
115g/4oz/1 cup diced Cheddar
   or mozzarella cheese
salt and freshly ground
   black pepper

**For the dressing**
45ml/3 tbsp red wine vinegar
   or balsamic vinegar
15ml/1 tbsp Dijon mustard
15ml/1 tbsp sesame seeds
60ml/4 tbsp olive oil
10ml/2 tsp chopped mixed
   fresh herbs

**1** Bring a large pan of lightly salted water to the boil and add the carrots and peas. Cook for 2 minutes, then add the broccoli. Cook until all the vegetables are crisp-tender.

**2** Using a slotted spoon, transfer the vegetables to a colander. Rinse under cold water. Drain. Tip into a bowl and set aside.

**3** Bring the water in the pan back to the boil. Add the pasta and cook until *al dente*. Drain, rinse under cold water, drain again and put into a large bowl. Add the oil, toss and leave until cold.

**4** Add the vegetable mixture to the pasta. Slice the pepper, celery, spring onions and tomato into small pieces. Add them to the bowl, with the olives.

**5** Make the dressing. Mix the vinegar, mustard and sesame seeds in a small bowl. Whisk in the oil, then add the herbs and mix lightly. Season to taste with salt and pepper.

**6** Pour the dressing over the salad and mix well. Stir in the diced cheese. Stand for 15 minutes before serving.

# Pasta Salad with Olives

This delicious salad combines the sunny flavours of the Mediterranean. Serve it with a radicchio and green leaf salad.

**Serves 6**

450g/1lb/4 cups dried, short
   pasta, such as conchiglie,
   farfalle or penne
60ml/4 tbsp extra virgin olive oil
10 sun-dried tomatoes,
   thinly sliced
30ml/2 tbsp bottled
   capers, drained
115g/4oz/1 cup pitted
   black olives
2 garlic cloves, finely chopped
45ml/3 tbsp balsamic vinegar
45ml/3 tbsp chopped
   fresh parsley
salt and freshly ground
   black pepper

**1** Bring a large pan of lightly salted water to the boil and cook the pasta until it is *al dente*. Drain, rinse under cold water and drain again. Tip it into a large bowl. Toss with the olive oil, then set aside.

**2** Soak the sun-dried tomatoes in a bowl of hot water for 10 minutes. Rinse the capers well. Drain the sun-dried tomatoes, reserving the soaking water.

**3** Combine the olives, tomatoes, capers, garlic and vinegar in a small bowl. Season to taste with salt and pepper.

**4** Stir this mixture into the pasta and toss well. Add 30–45ml/ 2–3 tbsp of the tomato soaking water if the salad seems too dry. Toss with the parsley, and leave to stand for about 15 minutes before serving.

> **Cook's Tip**
> Use capers preserved in salt, if you like, but soak them in hot water for 10 minutes first. Even better, use capers preserved in olive oil, if you can find them, and use some of the oil from the jar instead of the plain olive oil.

# Artichoke Pasta Salad

Marinated artichoke hearts make a delicious ingredient in a pasta salad, especially when peppers and broccoli add extra colour.

**Serves 4**

105ml/7 tbsp olive oil
1 red (bell) pepper, quartered,
   seeded and thinly sliced
1 onion, halved and thinly sliced
5ml/1 tsp dried thyme
45ml/3 tbsp sherry vinegar
450g/1lb dried penne or fusilli
2 x 175g/6oz jars marinated
   artichoke hearts, drained and
   thinly sliced
150g/5oz/1 cup cooked
   broccoli, chopped
20–25 salt-cured black olives,
   pitted and chopped
30ml/2 tbsp chopped
   fresh parsley
salt and freshly ground
   black pepper

**1** Heat 30ml/2 tbsp of the oil in a large, shallow pan. Add the red pepper and onion, and cook over a low heat, stirring occasionally, for 8–10 minutes, until just soft.

**2** Stir in the thyme, vinegar and 1.5ml/¼ tsp salt. Cook, stirring, for 30 seconds more, then set aside.

**3** Bring a large pan of lightly salted water to the boil and cook the pasta until it is *al dente*. Drain, rinse under cold water, then drain again and put in a large bowl. Add 30ml/2 tbsp of the remaining oil and toss well to coat.

**4** Add the onion mixture to the pasta, with the artichokes, broccoli, olives, parsley and remaining oil. Season with salt and pepper to taste. Stir to blend. Cover and leave to stand for at least 1 hour before serving, or place in the refrigerator overnight. Serve at room temperature.

> **Variation**
> Use whole baby artichokes in oil rather than artichoke hearts.

# Roquefort & Walnut Pasta Salad

This is a simple earthy salad, relying totally on the quality of the ingredients.

**Serves 4**
225g/8oz/2 cups dried
  pasta shapes
30ml/2 tbsp walnut oil
60ml/4 tbsp sunflower oil
30ml/2 tbsp red wine vinegar or
  sherry vinegar

selection of salad leaves, such as
  rocket (arugula), lamb's lettuce
  (corn salad), baby spinach
  and radicchio
225g/8oz Roquefort cheese,
  roughly crumbled
115g/4oz/1 cup walnut halves
salt and freshly ground
  black pepper

**1** Bring a large pan of lightly salted water to the boil and cook the pasta until it is *al dente*. Drain, rinse under cold water and drain again. Leave to cool.

**2** Make a dressing by whisking the walnut oil, sunflower oil and vinegar in a bowl. Season with salt and pepper to taste and whisk again.

**3** Arrange the salad leaves around the rim of a large salad bowl. Pile the pasta in the centre of the leaves, sprinkle over the crumbled Roquefort and pour over the dressing.

**4** Sprinkle over the walnuts. Toss the salad at the table, just before serving.

> **Cook's Tip**
> *Sherry vinegar has a full and rounded flavour that perfectly complements the cheese and nuts.*

> **Variation**
> *Try toasting the walnuts under the grill (broiler) for a couple of minutes to release their flavour.*

# Three Bean Pasta Salad

This hearty salad has a tangy yogurt dressing.

**Serves 3–4**
75g/3oz/ ¾ cup dried penne
2 tomatoes
200g/7oz can red kidney beans
200g/7oz can cannellini beans
200g/7oz can chickpeas

1 green (bell) pepper, seeded
  and diced
75ml/5 tbsp natural (plain) yogurt
30ml/2 tbsp sunflower oil
grated rind of ½ lemon
10ml/2 tsp wholegrain mustard
5ml/1 tsp chopped fresh oregano
salt and freshly ground
  black pepper

**1** Bring a large pan of lightly salted water to the boil and cook the pasta until it is *al dente*. Drain, rinse under cold water and drain again.

**2** Make a cross with the tip of a sharp knife in the blossom end of each of the tomatoes. Plunge them into a bowl of boiling water for 30 seconds. Remove with a slotted spoon or spatula, place in a bowl of cold water until cool enough to handle, then peel off the skins. Cut the tomatoes into segments.

**3** Drain the canned beans and chickpeas in a colander, rinse them under cold water and drain again. Tip into a bowl. Add the tomato segments, green pepper and pasta.

**4** In a separate bowl, whisk the yogurt until smooth. Gradually whisk in the oil, lemon rind and mustard. Stir in the oregano, and season with salt and pepper to taste. Pour the dressing over the salad and toss well. Serve immediately.

> **Variation**
> *This salad can be made with any of your favourite beans. Aduki, borlotti, flageolet (small cannellini) and lima beans are all good.*

# Noodle Salad with Sesame Oil Dressing

Toasted sesame oil adds a nutty flavour to this Asian-style salad. It is best served warm as a main course.

**Serves 2–4**
250g/9oz medium dried
    egg noodles
200g/7oz/1¾ cups mangetouts
    (snow peas), sliced diagonally
30ml/2 tbsp chopped fresh
    coriander (cilantro)
2 carrots, cut into
    fine strips
2 tomatoes, seeded and diced

15ml/1 tbsp sesame seeds
3 spring onions
    (scallions), shredded
salt
fresh coriander (cilantro),
    to garnish

**For the dressing**
10ml/2 tsp light soy sauce
30ml/2 tbsp toasted sesame
    seed oil
15ml/1 tbsp sunflower oil
4cm/1½in piece of fresh root
    ginger, finely grated
1 garlic clove, crushed

**1** Bring a pan of lightly salted water to the boil and cook the noodles for 2 minutes, then add the mangetouts and cook for 2 minutes more. Drain, rinse under cold water and drain again.

**2** Make the dressing. Combine the soy sauce, sesame and sunflower oils, ginger and garlic in a screw-top jar or bowl. Shake or mix to combine thoroughly.

**3** Tip the noodles and the mangetouts into a bowl and add the coriander, carrots and tomatoes. Pour the dressing over the top, and toss to combine. Sprinkle with the sesame seeds and top with the spring onions and coriander. Serve immediately.

**Cook's Tip**
*Clean hands are often the best implements for tossing salads. Less damaging than wooden servers, and warmer, they enable the cook to get a feel for what is being presented and ensure good distribution of the dressing.*

# Thamin Lethok

This is the Burmese way of dealing with leftovers and very successful it is too.

**Serves 6**
175g/6oz/scant 1 cup long
    grain rice
1–2 fresh red chillies, seeded and
    roughly chopped
1 small onion, roughly chopped
15ml/1 tbsp vegetable oil
2 potatoes, diced (optional)
115g/4oz dried egg noodles,
    soaked for 30 minutes in cold
    water to cover
115g/4oz dried rice noodles,
    soaked for at least 10 minutes
    in cold water to cover
50g/2oz cellophane noodles

225g/8oz spinach leaves
175g/6oz/3 cups beansprouts
25ml/1½ tbsp tamarind pulp,
    soaked in 200ml/7fl oz/scant
    1 cup warm water
salt

**For the accompaniments**
1 very small onion, thinly sliced
3 spring onions (scallions),
    finely shredded
crisp fried onion
50g/2oz cellophane noodles, fried
    until crisp
25g/1oz/2 tbsp chickpeas, dry-
    roasted and pounded
3 dried chillies, dry-fried
    and pounded
fresh coriander (cilantro) leaves

**1** Bring a pan of lightly salted water to the boil and cook the rice for 12–15 minutes, until tender. Drain and tip into a bowl. Pound the chillies with the onion in a mortar. Heat the oil in a pan, add the mixture and fry for 2–3 minutes. Set aside.

**2** Cook the potatoes in boiling salted water for 8–10 minutes, if using, until just tender; drain and set aside. Drain the noodles and cook them in separate pans of salted, boiling water until just tender. Drain, rinse under cold water and drain again.

**3** Put the spinach into a pan with just the water clinging to the leaves after washing. Cover and cook for 2 minutes. Drain well. Cook the beansprouts in the same way. Leave both to get cold.

**4** Arrange the cold flavoured rice, potato cubes, noodles, spinach and beansprouts attractively on a large serving platter. Set out the accompaniments. Strain the tamarind juice into a jug (pitcher). The guests help themselves to whatever they like.

# QUICK & EASY PASTA

It is likely that pasta and noodles can legitimately lay claim to being the original "fast food", as they both cook in a matter of minutes. However, this is no help to the busy cook – and who isn't these days – if the sauce to go with them is going to take ages to prepare. This chapter is packed with clever ideas for easy sauces, most of which take no longer than the pasta cooking time and, sometimes, even less. Simplicity and speed does not mean that you have to sacrifice flavour. Creamy cheeses, fresh herbs, crisp spring vegetables and sun-ripened summer tomatoes, (bell) peppers and courgettes (zucchini) are only some of the tasty ingredients that, combined with freshly cooked pasta, make an almost instant meal – perfect for midweek entertaining and family suppers. Inspiration for fast and flavour-packed noodle dishes comes from the food stalls that line the teeming streets of many South-east Asian cities. Without doubt, stir-frying is one of the quickest and easiest ways to cook, and vegetables are ideal for this technique, which retains their colour, texture, flavour and nutritional content. Within about ten minutes, you can conjure up a steaming-hot, aromatic dish of crisp-tender vegetables and succulent noodles, coated in a tangy sauce with just a hint of spice that could not be bettered if you had spent hours in the kitchen.

# Chitarra Spaghetti with Butter & Herbs

This is a versatile recipe. You can use just one favourite herb or several – basil, flat leaf parsley, rosemary, thyme, marjoram or sage would all work well. The square-shaped *spaghetti alla chitarra* is traditional with this kind of sauce, but you could use ordinary spaghetti or even linguine.

**Serves 4**
*2 good handfuls of mixed fresh herbs, plus extra herb leaves and flowers, to garnish*
*400g/14oz fresh or dried spaghetti alla chitarra*
*115g/4oz/ ½ cup butter*
*salt and freshly ground black pepper*
*freshly grated Parmesan cheese, to serve*

**1** Chop the herbs roughly or finely, whichever you like.

**2** Bring a large pan of lightly salted water to the boil and cook the pasta until it is *al dente*.

**3** When the pasta is almost ready, melt the butter in a large, heavy pan. As soon as it sizzles, drain the pasta and add it to the pan, then sprinkle in the herbs and season with salt and pepper to taste.

**4** Toss over a medium heat until the pasta is coated in the butter and herbs. Serve immediately in warmed bowls, sprinkled with extra herb leaves and flowers. Hand around freshly grated Parmesan separately.

> **Variation**
> *If you like the flavour of garlic with herbs, add one to two crushed garlic cloves when melting the butter.*

# Fusilli with Basil & Parsley

Choose a mixture of plain, spinach and tomato pasta for this recipe.

**Serves 4**
*400g/14oz dried fusilli*

**For the basil and parsley sauce**
*2 garlic cloves, crushed*
*75g/3oz/1 cup pine nuts*
*50g/2oz/2 cups fresh basil leaves, plus extra to garnish*
*25g/1oz/ ½ cup fresh flat leaf parsley*
*150ml/ ¼ pint/ ⅔ cup extra virgin olive oil*
*salt and freshly ground black pepper*

**1** Bring a large pan of lightly salted water to the boil and cook the pasta until *al dente*.

**2** Meanwhile, make the sauce. Place the garlic, pine nuts, basil and parsley in a blender or food processor. Process briefly to chop and mix. With the motor running, gradually add the olive oil through the lid or feeder tube. Continue to process until the sauce is smooth and creamy.

**3** Drain the pasta and return it to the clean pan. Toss well with the sauce, and season to taste with salt and pepper. Serve in warmed bowls, garnished with extra fresh basil leaves.

> **Cook's Tip**
> *The basil and parsley sauce can be made in advance and will keep for a few days in the refrigerator.*

> **Variation**
> *You can vary the flavour of the sauce by using fresh coriander (cilantro) instead of the parsley.*

# Garlic & Herb Pasta

Served with plenty of fresh Parmesan cheese, this tasty pasta dish makes a speedy and satisfying supper.

**Serves 4**
250g/9oz mixed dried egg and spinach tagliatelle
3 garlic cloves, crushed
30ml/2 tbsp drained capers, finely chopped
10ml/2 tsp Dijon mustard
60ml/4 tbsp olive oil
60ml/4 tbsp mixed chopped fresh chives, parsley and oregano
50g/2oz/ ½ cup pine nuts, toasted
15ml/1 tbsp lemon juice
salt and freshly ground black pepper
freshly shaved Parmesan cheese, to serve

**1** Bring a large pan of lightly salted water to the boil and cook the pasta until *al dente*.

**2** Mix the garlic, capers and mustard in a bowl. Gradually drizzle in the olive oil, whisking constantly until thoroughly combined. Stir in the herbs, pine nuts and lemon juice. Season with salt and plenty of pepper.

**3** Drain the pasta and return it to the clean pan. Add the herb dressing and toss until well combined. Serve in warmed bowls, sprinkled with plenty of shaved Parmesan cheese.

---

**Variations**
• You can use the classic combination of fines herbes – parsley, chervil, tarragon and chives instead of the mixed herbs suggested here.
• For a very herby flavour, if you can get it, serve with grated Sapsago, which is flavoured with melilot.

---

# Tagliatelle with Fresh Herbs

This is a lovely dish for a light summer lunch when fresh herbs are plentiful.

**Serves 4**
3 fresh rosemary sprigs
1 small handful of fresh flat leaf parsley
5–6 fresh mint leaves
5–6 fresh sage leaves
8–10 large fresh basil leaves, plus extra to garnish
30ml/2 tbsp extra virgin olive oil
50g/2oz/ ¼ cup butter
1 shallot, finely chopped
2 garlic cloves, finely chopped
pinch of chilli powder
400g/14oz fresh egg tagliatelle
1 bay leaf
120ml/4fl oz/ ½ cup dry white wine
90–120ml/6–8 tbsp Vegetable Stock
salt and freshly ground black pepper

**1** Strip the rosemary and parsley leaves from their stalks and chop them with the fresh mint, sage and basil.

**2** Heat the olive oil and half the butter in a large, heavy pan. Add the shallot and garlic, and season with chilli powder to taste. Cook over a very low heat, stirring frequently, for 2–3 minutes.

**3** Meanwhile, bring a large pan of lightly salted water to the boil and cook the pasta until *al dente*.

**4** Add the chopped herbs and the bay leaf to the shallot mixture and stir for 2–3 minutes. Increase the heat, add the wine and bring to the boil, then boil rapidly for 1–2 minutes until it reduces. Lower the heat, add the vegetable stock and simmer for 1–2 minutes.

**5** Drain the pasta and add it to the herb mixture. Toss well to mix, then remove and discard the bay leaf. Season to taste with salt and pepper.

**6** Put the remaining butter in a warmed large bowl, tip the dressed pasta into it and toss thoroughly to mix until the butter has melted. Serve immediately, garnished with basil leaves.

# Pasta from Pisa

Nothing could be simpler than hot pasta tossed with fresh ripe tomatoes, ricotta and sweet basil. Serve it on a hot summer's day, as it is surprisingly refreshing.

**Serves 4–6**
350g/12oz/3 cups
   dried conchiglie
130g/4½oz/⅔ cup
   ricotta cheese

2 garlic cloves, crushed
a handful of fresh basil leaves,
   shredded, plus extra basil
   leaves to garnish
6 ripe Italian plum tomatoes,
   diced small
60ml/4 tbsp extra virgin olive oil
salt and freshly ground
   black pepper

**1** Bring a large pan of lightly salted water to the boil and cook the pasta until it is *al dente*.

**2** Meanwhile, put the ricotta in a large bowl and mash it with a fork until smooth.

**3** Add the garlic and basil, season with salt and pepper to taste and mix well. Add the olive oil and whisk thoroughly. Add the tomatoes and taste for seasoning.

**4** Drain the cooked pasta, tip it into the ricotta and tomato mixture and toss thoroughly to mix. Garnish with extra basil leaves and serve immediately.

---

### Variations
• An avocado is the ideal ingredient for adding extra colour and flavour to this pasta dish. Halve, stone (pit) and peel, then dice the flesh. Toss it with the hot pasta at the last minute to avoid discoloration of the flesh.
• Substitute diced mozzarella cheese for the ricotta and garnish with black olives.
• Use fresh mint leaves instead of the basil.

---

# Penne with Rocket & Mozzarella

Like a warm salad, this pasta dish is very quick and easy to make – perfect for an *al fresco* summer lunch.

**Serves 4**
400g/14oz/3½ cups fresh or
   dried penne
6 ripe Italian plum tomatoes,
   peeled, seeded and diced

2 x 150g/5oz packets mozzarella
   cheese, drained and diced
4 large handfuls of rocket
   (arugula), total weight
   about 150g/5oz
75ml/5 tbsp extra virgin olive oil
salt and freshly ground
   black pepper

**1** Bring a large pan of lightly salted water to the boil and cook the pasta until it is *al dente*.

**2** Meanwhile, put the tomatoes, mozzarella, rocket and olive oil into a large bowl, season with a little salt and pepper to taste, and toss well to mix.

**3** Drain the cooked pasta and tip it into the bowl. Toss well to mix and serve immediately.

---

### Cook's Tip
As with all simple recipes, the success of this dish depends upon having the freshest and best-quality ingredients. It is worth looking for mozzarella di bufala. Make sure that you buy only tender young rocket (arugula) with no yellowing or damaged leaves. Sun-ripened tomatoes have the sweetest flavour; if in doubt about the quality, buy vine tomatoes.

---

### Variation
Unless the rocket (arugula) leaves are very young, they can be quite peppery. For a less peppery taste, use basil leaves instead of rocket, or a mixture of the two.

# Garganelli with Spring Vegetables

A light, buttery sauce marries young fresh vegetables and pasta to make a dish that would be ideal for a simple lunch.

**Serves 4**

350g/12oz fresh young
  asparagus, trimmed
4 young carrots
1 bunch spring onions (scallions)
150g/5oz/1¼ cups shelled
  fresh peas
350g/12oz/3 cups
  dried garganelli
75g/3oz/6 tbsp unsalted (sweet)
  butter, diced
60ml/4 tbsp dry white wine
a few sprigs each of fresh flat leaf
  parsley, mint and basil, leaves
  stripped and chopped
salt and freshly ground
  black pepper
freshly grated Parmesan cheese,
  to serve

**1** Cut off the asparagus tips, holding the knife at a slant. Set the tips aside. Cut the stems on the diagonal into 4cm/1½in pieces.

**2** Cut the carrots and spring onions on the diagonal into 4cm/1½in pieces.

**3** Bring a large pan of lightly salted water to the boil and add the asparagus stems, carrots and peas. Bring back to the boil, then simmer for 5 minutes. Add the asparagus tips and simmer for 3 minutes more. Using a slotted spoon, transfer the cooked vegetables to a bowl.

**4** Bring the water used for cooking the vegetables back to the boil and cook the pasta until it is *al dente*.

**5** Meanwhile, melt the butter in a large, heavy frying pan. Add the cooked vegetables, with the white wine, and season with salt and pepper to taste. Toss over a medium to high heat until the wine has reduced and the vegetables are glistening with melted butter.

**6** Drain the pasta and tip it into a warmed large bowl. Add the dressed vegetables, the spring onions and the herbs and toss well. Serve immediately, with freshly grated Parmesan.

# Capellini with Rocket & Mangetouts

A light but filling pasta dish, with the added pepperiness of fresh rocket.

**Serves 4**

250g/9oz dried capellini
225g/8oz mangetouts
  (snow peas)
175g/6oz rocket (arugula)
50g/2oz/½ cup pine
  nuts, roasted
30ml/2 tbsp freshly grated
  Parmesan cheese
salt and freshly ground
  black pepper

**1** Bring a large pan of lightly salted water to the boil and cook the pasta until *al dente*. Meanwhile, carefully trim the mangetouts.

**2** As soon as the pasta is cooked, drop the rocket and mangetouts into the pan. Drain immediately.

**3** Tip the pasta mixture into a warmed bowl, and add the pine nuts and Parmesan. Season and toss to coat. Serve immediately.

# Capellini with Spinach & Feta

An ideal supper dish for warm evenings when you don't feel much like cooking.

**Serves 6**

375g/12oz dried capellini
300g/11oz mangetouts
  (snow peas)
275g/10oz baby spinach leaves
30ml/2 tbsp chopped fresh
  oregano or marjoram
115g/4oz feta cheese, crumbled
salt and freshly ground
  black pepper

**1** Bring a large pan of lightly salted water to the boil and cook the pasta until *al dente*. Meanwhile, trim the mangetouts.
**2** As soon as the pasta is cooked, drop the spinach and mangetouts into the pan, then drain immediately.
**3** Tip the pasta mixture into a warmed bowl and add the oregano or marjoram and feta. Season, toss well and serve.

# Conchiglie with Tomatoes & Rocket

This pretty pasta dish owes its success to the contrast in flavour between sweet cherry tomatoes and peppery rocket.

**Serves 4**
450g/1lb/4 cups dried conchiglie
    or farfalle
45ml/3 tbsp olive oil
450g/1lb ripe cherry
    tomatoes, halved
75g/3oz fresh rocket (arugula)
salt and freshly ground
    black pepper
freshly shaved Parmesan cheese,
    to serve

**1** Bring a large pan of lightly salted water to the boil and cook the pasta until it is *al dente*.

**2** Heat the oil in a pan, add the tomatoes and cook for barely 1 minute. The tomatoes should only just heat through and not disintegrate.

**3** Trim the rocket, removing any tough stems. Wash the leaves, drain well, then pat them dry with kitchen paper.

**4** Drain the pasta, return it to the clean pan and add the tomatoes, then the rocket. Carefully stir over the heat to mix and heat through. Season well with salt and pepper. Serve immediately with plenty of shaved Parmesan cheese.

**Variations**
• Cut four unpeeled red potatoes into eight pieces and cook with the pasta, omitting the tomatoes.
• Instead of rocket (arugula), use 115g/4oz radicchio di Treviso or 75g/3oz lamb's lettuce (also known as corn salad) or 115g/4oz spinach.

# Double Tomato Tagliatelle

Sun-dried tomatoes add pungency to this dish, while the grilled fresh tomatoes give it bite.

**Serves 4**
45ml/3 tbsp olive oil
1 garlic clove, crushed
1 small onion, chopped
60ml/4 tbsp dry white wine
6 drained sun-dried tomatoes in
    oil, chopped
30ml/2 tbsp chopped
    fresh parsley
50g/2oz/ 1/2 cup pitted
    black olives, halved
4 tomatoes, halved
450g/1lb fresh tagliatelle
salt and freshly ground
    black pepper
freshly shaved Parmesan cheese,
    to serve

**1** Heat 30ml/2 tbsp of the olive oil in a large, heavy pan. Add the garlic and onion, and cook over a medium heat, stirring occasionally, for 2–3 minutes, until softened.

**2** Stir in the wine, sun-dried tomatoes and parsley. Cook for 2 minutes. Stir in the black olives.

**3** Preheat the grill (broiler). Put the tomatoes on a tray and brush them with the remaining oil. Grill (broil) under a medium heat until cooked through and beginning to brown on top.

**4** Meanwhile, bring a large pan of lightly salted water to the boil and cook the tagliatelle until *al dente*.

**5** Drain the pasta, return it to the clean pan and toss with the sauce. Serve with the grilled tomatoes, freshly ground black pepper and shavings of Parmesan.

**Cook's Tip**
Olives marinated in olive oil flavoured with garlic and herbs would go especially well in this dish, but olives in brine are also satisfactory. Spanish and Greek black olives tend to be plumper and juicier than Italian.

# Pasta with Sugocasa & Chilli

Sugocasa consists of crushed Italian tomatoes and comes in bottles or jars. It is coarser than passata, but finer than canned chopped tomatoes and is ideal for quick dishes, such as this one.

**Serves 4**
500g/1lb sugocasa
2 garlic cloves, crushed
150ml/ ¼ pint/ ⅔ cup dry
  white wine
15ml/1 tbsp sun-dried
  tomato purée (paste)
1 fresh red chilli
350g/12oz dried pasta tubes
  such as macaroni or penne
60ml/4 tbsp finely chopped fresh
  flat leaf parsley
salt and freshly ground
  black pepper
freshly grated Pecorino cheese,
  to serve

**1** Put the sugocasa, garlic, wine, sun-dried tomato purée and whole chilli in a pan and bring to the boil. Cover, lower the heat and simmer gently.

**2** Bring a large pan of lightly salted water to the boil, add the pasta and cook until al dente.

**3** Remove the chilli from the sauce. If you want a mere suggestion of heat, discard it. Otherwise, seed and chop some or all of the flesh and return it to the sauce. Stir in half the parsley. Taste for seasoning.

**4** Drain the pasta and tip it into a warmed large bowl. Pour the sauce over the pasta and toss to mix. Serve immediately, sprinkled with the grated Pecorino and the remaining parsley.

**Cook's Tip**
*Look for sugocasa in delicatessens or supermarkets. It is sometimes labelled "crushed Italian tomatoes". If you can't locate it, use a mixture of canned chopped tomatoes and passata (bottled strained tomatoes) instead.*

# Penne with Tomatoes & Mozzarella

This is a deliciously light pasta dish, full of fresh flavours. Use buffalo-milk mozzarella, if you can – its flavour is noticeably better.

**Serves 4**
275g/10oz/2½ cups dried penne
450g/1lb ripe plum tomatoes
275g/10oz mozzarella
  cheese, drained
60ml/4 tbsp olive oil
15ml/1 tbsp balsamic vinegar
grated rind of 1 lemon
15ml/1 tbsp lemon juice
15 fresh basil leaves, shredded,
  plus extra, to garnish
salt and freshly ground
  black pepper

**1** Bring a large pan of lightly salted water to the boil and cook the pasta until al dente.

**2** Meanwhile, cut the tomatoes into quarters and squeeze out the seeds, then chop the flesh into cubes. Cut the mozzarella into pieces of a similar size.

**3** Put the olive oil in a bowl and stir in the balsamic vinegar, lemon rind, lemon juice and basil. Stir well, then season with salt and pepper to taste. Add the tomatoes and mozzarella, and leave to stand until the pasta is cooked.

**4** Drain the pasta and return it to the clean pan. Add the tomato mixture and toss well. Garnish with the extra basil leaves and serve immediately, if serving hot, or allow to cool to room temperature.

**Variation**
*Add 50g/2oz/ ½ cup black olives and 25g/1oz/ ½ cup chopped, drained sun-dried tomatoes in oil with the fresh tomatoes in step 3. Proceed as the recipe above and serve garnished with 30ml/2 tbsp toasted pine nuts.*

# Spaghetti with Sun-dried Tomato Sauce

There's something totally irresistible about sun-dried tomatoes. All that rich, concentrated, fruity flavour makes them ideal for serving with spaghetti.

**Serves 4**

350g/12oz dried spaghetti
4 garlic cloves, crushed
10–15 sun-dried tomatoes
   in oil, drained and
   roughly chopped
50g/2oz/½ cup pitted
   black olives
120ml/4fl oz/ ½ cup extra virgin
   olive oil
3 beefsteak tomatoes, peeled,
   seeded and chopped
45ml/3 tbsp drained capers
25g/1oz/ ¼ cup chopped fresh
   basil, plus extra leaves
   to garnish
salt and freshly ground
   black pepper

**1** Bring a large pan of lightly salted water to the boil and cook the spaghetti until *al dente*.

**2** Meanwhile, put the garlic, sun-dried tomatoes and the olives in a food processor or blender. Process until finely chopped. With the motor running, slowly add the olive oil through the hole in the lid or the feeder tube. Continue processing until thickened and smooth.

**3** Scrape the mixture into a mixing bowl. Stir in the chopped fresh tomatoes, capers and chopped basil. Season with salt and pepper to taste.

**4** Drain the spaghetti well, return it to the clean pan and add the tomato sauce. Toss well. Serve in warmed bowls, garnished with fresh basil leaves.

### Cook's Tip
*You can replace some of the olive oil with a little of the oil from the tomatoes for a stronger flavour.*

# Spirali with Tomato & Cream Cheese Sauce

Treat the family with this inexpensive, easy, but very tasty pasta dish.

**Serves 4**

30ml/2 tbsp olive oil
1 red onion, thinly sliced
2 garlic cloves, chopped
200g/7oz jar sun-dried tomatoes
   in oil, drained
30ml/2 tbsp roughly chopped
   fresh herbs
400g/14oz can
   chopped tomatoes
350g/12oz dried spirali
60ml/4 tbsp cream cheese
salt and freshly ground
   black pepper
chopped fresh flat leaf parsley,
   to garnish

**1** Heat the oil in a frying pan and cook the onion, stirring occasionally, for 5 minutes, until slightly softened. Stir in the garlic and sun-dried tomatoes, and cook for 2–3 minutes more. Add the herbs and canned tomatoes and bring to the boil. Simmer over a low heat until the sauce has thickened.

**2** Meanwhile, bring a large pan of lightly salted water to the boil and cook the pasta until it is *al dente*.

**3** Add the cream cheese and seasoning to the sauce and stir over a medium heat until it is well combined.

**4** Drain the pasta and return it to the clean pan. Add the sauce and toss to coat. Serve in warmed bowls, garnished with chopped flat leaf parsley.

### Cook's Tip
*Cut the cost of using sun-dried tomatoes in oil. Buy a large bag of dry sun-dried tomatoes from a health-food shop. Soak them overnight in water to cover. Squeeze out the excess moisture, then put them in a jar and cover with virgin olive oil. Add sliced garlic and fresh herbs for extra flavour and cover with an airtight lid. These will keep for several months in the refrigerator.*

# Linguine with Sun-dried Tomato Pesto

Tomato pesto was once a rarity, but is becoming increasingly popular and is absolutely delicious.

**Serves 4**

25g/1oz/ 1/3 cup pine nuts
25g/1oz/ 1/3 cup freshly grated
   Parmesan cheese
50g/2oz/ 1/2 cup drained sun-
   dried tomatoes in olive oil
1 garlic clove, roughly chopped
60ml/4 tbsp olive oil
350g/12oz fresh or dried linguine
salt and freshly ground black pepper
basil leaves, to garnish
coarsely shaved Parmesan cheese,
   to serve

**1** Put the pine nuts in a small non-stick frying pan and toss them over a low to medium heat for 1–2 minutes, or until they are lightly toasted and golden.

**2** Tip the nuts into a food processor. Add the Parmesan, sun-dried tomatoes and garlic with pepper to taste. Process until finely chopped. With the machine running, gradually add the olive oil through the feeder tube until it has all been incorporated evenly and the mixture is smooth.

**3** Bring a large pan of lightly salted water to the boil and cook the pasta until it is *al dente*.

**4** Drain the pasta, reserving 60ml/4 tbsp of the cooking water. Tip the pasta into a warmed bowl, add the pesto and the hot water and toss well. Serve in warmed bowls, garnished with basil leaves. Hand round shavings of Parmesan separately.

> **Cook's Tip**
> *You can make this pesto up to 2 days in advance and keep it in a bowl in the refrigerator until ready to use. Pour a thin film of olive oil over the pesto in the bowl, then cover the bowl tightly with clear film (plastic wrap) to prevent the strong smell of the pesto from tainting other foods in the refrigerator.*

# Vermicelli with Lemon

Fresh and tangy, this is a good recipe to remember when you're pushed for time, because the sauce can be made in the time it takes to cook the pasta.

**Serves 4**

350g/12oz dried vermicelli
juice of 2 large lemons
50g/2oz/ 1/4 cup butter
200ml/7fl oz/scant 1 cup
   double (heavy) cream
115g/4oz/1 1/3 cups freshly grated
   Parmesan cheese, plus extra
   to serve
salt and freshly ground
   black pepper

**1** Bring a large pan of lightly salted water to the boil and cook the pasta until it is *al dente*.

**2** Meanwhile, pour the lemon juice into a heavy medium pan. Add the butter and cream, then season with salt and pepper to taste.

**3** Bring to the boil, then lower the heat and simmer for about 5 minutes, stirring occasionally, until the cream reduces slightly.

**4** Drain the pasta and return it to the clean pan. Add the grated Parmesan, then pour over the sauce. Toss quickly over a medium heat until the pasta is evenly coated with the sauce, then divide the mixture among four warmed bowls and serve immediately. Hand extra grated Parmesan separately.

> **Cook's Tips**
> • *Lemons vary in the amount of juice they yield. On average, a large fresh lemon will yield 60–90ml/4–6 tbsp. This dish is quite tangy; you can use less juice if you like.*
> • *A lemon at room temperature will yield more juice than one straight from the refrigerator.*
> • *For an even more lemony taste, you could add a little grated lemon rind to the sauce when you add the butter and cream to the pan in step 2.*

# Fusilli with Mascarpone & Spinach

Simply delicious – that sums up this combination of a creamy, green sauce with tender pasta.

**Serves 4**
350g/12oz/3 cups dried fusilli
50g/2oz/ ¼ cup butter
1 onion, chopped
1 garlic clove, chopped
30ml/2 tbsp fresh thyme leaves
225g/8oz frozen leaf spinach,
   thawed and drained
225g/8oz/1 cup
   mascarpone cheese
salt and freshly ground
   black pepper
fresh thyme sprigs, to garnish

**1** Bring a large pan of lightly salted water to the boil and cook the pasta until it is *al dente*.

**2** Meanwhile, melt the butter in a large, heavy pan. Add the onion and fry over a low heat, stirring occasionally, for 4–5 minutes, until softened.

**3** Stir in the garlic, thyme and spinach, and season with salt and pepper to taste. Heat gently, stirring occasionally, for about 5 minutes, until heated through.

**4** Stir in the mascarpone and heat gently until melted and heated through.

**5** Drain the pasta thoroughly and return it to the clean pan. Add the sauce and toss until well coated. Serve immediately, garnished with the fresh thyme.

### Variations
*Use a mixture of cheeses instead of plain mascarpone. Mash together equal quantities of mascarpone and Gorgonzola or Roquefort or mix together equal quantities of mascarpone and grated Parmesan or Pecorino. Alternatively, replace the mascarpone with torta di Gorgonzola, which consists of layers of Gorgonzola and mascarpone.*

# Tagliatelle with Mozzarella & Asparagus Sauce

Tender asparagus tips look very impressive surrounded by ribbons of tender pasta.

**Serves 4**
225g/8oz asparagus tips
350g/12oz dried tagliatelle
115g/4oz/ ½ cup butter
1 onion, chopped
1 garlic clove, chopped
30ml/2 tbsp Vegetable Stock
   or water
150ml/ ¼ pint/ ⅔ cup
   double (heavy) cream
75g/3oz mozzarella
   cheese, grated
salt and freshly ground
   black pepper
fresh flat leaf parsley sprigs,
   to garnish

**1** Bring a large pan of lightly salted water to the boil. Add the fresh asparagus and cook for 5–10 minutes, until tender. Lift out the asparagus tips with a slotted spoon and set them aside.

**2** Bring the pan of water back to the boil and cook the pasta until it is *al dente*.

**3** Meanwhile, melt the butter in a large frying pan and fry the onion with the garlic over a low heat for 5 minutes, until softened. Stir in the stock or water.

**4** Pour in the cream and bring to the boil, stirring. Add the asparagus. Simmer for 2 minutes, stirring occasionally.

**5** Add the mozzarella cheese and simmer for 1 minute more. Season with salt and pepper to taste.

**6** Drain the pasta and tip it into a warmed bowl. Add the sauce and toss to coat. Serve immediately, garnished with the parsley.

### Cook's Tip
*Fresh asparagus is still quite seasonal, so keep your eyes open for it and cook it in this delicious sauce when it is at its best.*

# Spaghetti with Pepper & Tomato Sauce

Keep an eye open for packs of mixed peppers, which are ideal for making this easy supper dish.

**Serves 4**

30ml/2 tbsp olive oil
2 onions, chopped
1 red (bell) pepper, seeded and cut into strips
1 green (bell) pepper, seeded and cut into strips
1 yellow (bell) pepper, seeded and cut into strips
3 tomatoes, peeled, seeded and chopped
1 garlic clove, chopped
15ml/1 tbsp chopped fresh oregano
350g/12oz dried spaghetti
salt and freshly ground black pepper
fresh oregano sprigs, to garnish

**1** Heat the oil in a large, heavy pan. Add the onions and peppers, and fry over a medium heat, stirring frequently, for 10 minutes, until softened.

**2** Stir in the tomatoes, garlic and chopped oregano. Season with plenty of salt and pepper, and bring to the boil, stirring frequently. Lower the heat and leave to simmer while you cook the pasta.

**3** Bring a large pan of lightly salted water to the boil and cook the pasta until it is *al dente*.

**4** Drain the pasta thoroughly and return it to the clean pan. Add the sauce and toss well. Serve immediately, garnished with the oregano sprigs.

> **Cook's Tip**
> For an even quicker sauce, use already cut (bell) pepper strips that you can buy in jars of olive oil. Fry the chopped onion for 3–5 minutes in step 1, then drain the peppers and add them in step 2.

# Strozzapreti with Courgette Flowers

This pretty, summery dish is strewn with colourful courgette flowers, but you can make it even if you don't have the flowers.

**Serves 4**

50g/2oz/¼ cup butter
30ml/2 tbsp extra virgin olive oil
1 small onion, thinly sliced
200g/7oz small courgettes (zucchini), cut into thin julienne
1 garlic clove, crushed
10ml/2 tsp finely chopped fresh marjoram
350g/12oz/3 cups dried strozzapreti
a large handful of courgette (zucchini) flowers, thoroughly washed and dried
salt and freshly ground black pepper
thin shavings of Parmesan cheese, to serve

**1** Heat the butter and half the olive oil in a pan and cook the onion over a low heat, stirring occasionally, until softened. Add the courgettes, garlic and marjoram and season with salt and pepper to taste. Mix well. Cook for 5–8 minutes until the courgettes have softened but are not coloured, turning them over from time to time.

**2** Meanwhile, bring a pan of lightly salted water to the boil and cook the pasta until it is *al dente*.

**3** Set aside a few whole courgette flowers for the garnish, then roughly shred the rest and add them to the courgette mixture. Stir to mix and taste for seasoning.

**4** Drain the pasta, tip it into a warmed large bowl and add the remaining oil. Toss thoroughly, add the courgette mixture and toss again. Top with Parmesan and the reserved courgette flowers and serve immediately.

> **Cook's Tip**
> Strozzapreti or "priest stranglers" are short pasta shapes from Modena. You can buy packets of them in Italian delicatessens, or use gemelli, a similar kind of twisted pasta.

# Thai Vegetables with Noodles

Serve this as a vegetarian supper on its own or as an accompaniment.

**Serves 4**

225g/8oz dried egg noodles
15ml/1 tbsp sesame oil
45ml/3 tbsp groundnut
  (peanut) oil
2 garlic cloves, thinly sliced
2.5cm/1in piece of fresh root
  ginger, finely chopped
2 fresh red chillies, seeded
  and sliced

115g/4oz broccoli, broken into
  small florets
115g/4oz/ ⅔ cup baby corn cobs
175g/6oz/2 cups shiitake
  mushrooms, sliced
1 bunch spring onions
  (scallions), sliced
115g/4oz pak choi (bok
  choy), shredded
115g/4oz/2 cups beansprouts
15–30ml/1–2 tbsp dark
  soy sauce
salt and freshly ground
  black pepper

**1** Bring a large pan of lightly salted water to the boil and cook the noodles briefly until just tender. Drain them thoroughly, tip them into a bowl and toss them with the sesame oil. Set aside.

**2** Preheat a wok, add the groundnut oil and swirl it around. Add the garlic and ginger, and stir-fry over a medium heat for 1 minute. Add the chillies, broccoli, corn cobs and mushrooms, and stir-fry for 2 minutes more.

**3** Add the spring onions, shredded pak choi and beansprouts, and stir-fry for another 2 minutes. Add the drained noodles with the soy sauce and pepper to taste.

**4** Toss the mixture over a high heat for 2–3 minutes, until the ingredients are well mixed and have heated through. Transfer to a warmed serving dish and serve immediately.

> **Variations**
> • If you like, you can use shredded Chinese cabbage instead of pak choi (bok choy).
> • Substitute oyster mushrooms for the shiitake.

# Sesame Noodles with Spring Onions

This simple but very tasty dish can be prepared and cooked in a few minutes.

**Serves 4**

2 garlic cloves, roughly chopped
30ml/2 tbsp Chinese
  sesame paste
15ml/1 tbsp dark sesame oil
30ml/2 tbsp soy sauce
30ml/2 tbsp Chinese rice wine or
  dry sherry

15ml/1 tbsp clear honey
a pinch of Chinese five-
  spice powder
350g/12oz dried noodles
4 spring onions (scallions), thinly
  sliced diagonally
50g/2oz/1 cup beansprouts
7.5cm/3in piece of cucumber, cut
  into thin batons
15ml/1 tbsp toasted sesame seeds
salt and freshly ground
  black pepper

**1** Put the garlic, sesame paste, sesame oil, soy sauce, Chinese rice wine or sherry, honey and five-spice powder with a pinch each of salt and pepper in a blender or food processor. Process until smooth.

**2** Bring a large pan of lightly salted water to the boil and cook the noodles briefly until just tender. Drain the noodles and tip them into a warmed serving bowl.

**3** Add the garlic and sesame paste to the hot noodles, with the spring onions, and toss to coat. Top with the beansprouts, cucumber and sesame seeds and serve.

> **Variation**
> If you can't find Chinese sesame paste, use tahini paste, available from supermarkets and delicatessens, or use smooth peanut butter instead.

# Noodles with Braised Leaves

Use Chinese leaves (Chinese cabbage) or white cabbage for this tasty dish.

**Serves 4**

225g/8oz dried egg noodles
5ml/1 tsp sesame oil
45ml/3 tbsp groundnut
  (peanut) oil

6 dried red chillies, seeded
  and chopped
2.5ml/ ½ tsp Sichuan
  peppercorns
450g/1lb Chinese leaves (Chinese
  cabbage), coarsely shredded
15ml/1 tbsp rice vinegar
15ml/1 tbsp granulated sugar
15ml/1 tbsp light soy sauce
salt

**1** Bring a pan of lightly salted water to the boil and cook the noodles briefly until they are just tender. Drain them well, then tip into a bowl and toss them with the sesame oil. Set aside.

**2** Heat the groundnut oil in a preheated wok and stir-fry the chillies and Sichuan peppercorns for 15 seconds. Add the Chinese leaves and stir-fry for about 1 minute. Season to taste with a pinch of salt and stir-fry for 1 further minute.

**3** Stir in the vinegar, sugar, soy sauce and noodles, and stir over the heat for 1 minute, until piping hot. Serve immediately.

# Stir-fried Beancurd with Noodles

This is a satisfying dish, which is both tasty and easy to make. It looks and smells wonderfully appetizing and will quickly become a firm family favourite.

**Serves 4**

225g/8oz firm beancurd (tofu)
groundnut (peanut) oil, for
    deep-frying
175g/6oz medium dried
    egg noodles
15ml/1 tbsp sesame oil
5ml/1 tsp cornflour (cornstarch)
10ml/2 tsp dark soy sauce
30ml/2 tbsp Chinese rice wine or
    dry sherry
5ml/1 tsp granulated sugar
6–8 spring onions (scallions),
    cut diagonally into 2.5cm/
    1in lengths
3 garlic cloves, sliced
1 fresh green chilli, seeded
    and sliced
115g/4oz Chinese cabbage
    leaves, coarsely shredded
50g/2oz/1 cup beansprouts
50g/2oz/ 1/2 cup cashew
    nuts, toasted

**1** Pat the beancurd dry with kitchen paper then cut it into 2.5cm/1in cubes. Half-fill a wok with groundnut oil and heat to 180°C/350°F or until a cube of day-old bread browns in 30 seconds. Deep-fry the beancurd cubes, in batches, for 1–2 minutes, until golden and crisp. Drain on kitchen paper. Carefully pour all but 30ml/2 tbsp of the oil from the wok.

**2** Bring a large pan of lightly salted water to the boil and cook the noodles briefly until they are just tender. Rinse them under cold water and drain well. Put them in a bowl, add 10ml/2 tsp of the sesame oil and toss to coat. Set aside.

**3** In a bowl, mix the cornflour with the soy sauce, rice wine or sherry, sugar and remaining sesame oil.

**4** Reheat the oil in the wok and add the spring onions, garlic, chilli, Chinese cabbage and beansprouts. Stir-fry over a medium heat for 1–2 minutes.

**5** Add the beancurd with the noodles and sauce. Cook, stirring constantly, for about 1 minute, until well mixed. Sprinkle over the cashew nuts. Serve immediately.

# Teriyaki Soba Noodles

Japanese soba noodles are made from buckwheat flour, which gives them a unique texture and colour. They are excellent with tofu and asparagus.

**Serves 4**

350g/12oz dried soba noodles
45ml/3 tbsp vegetable oil
200g/7oz asparagus tips
10ml/2 tsp sesame oil
225g/8oz block of firm tofu
2 spring onions (scallions), cut into
    thin strips
1 carrot, cut into thin batons
2.5ml/ 1/2 tsp dried chilli flakes
15ml/1 tbsp sesame seeds
salt and freshly ground
    black pepper

**For the teriyaki sauce**
60ml/4 tbsp dark soy sauce
60ml/4 tbsp Japanese sake or
    dry sherry
60ml/4 tbsp mirin
5ml/1 tsp caster (superfine) sugar

**1** Bring a large pan of lightly salted water to the boil and cook the soba noodles briefly until they are just tender. Drain, rinse under cold running water and drain again.

**2** Heat about 30ml/2 tbsp of the vegetable oil in a griddle pan and cook the asparagus for 8–10 minutes, turning frequently, until tender and browned. Using tongs, transfer to a bowl and toss with the sesame oil.

**3** Preheat a wok. Swirl in the remaining vegetable oil. When it is very hot, add the tofu and fry for 8–10 minutes, until golden and crisp on all sides. Carefully lift it out of the wok and leave it to drain on kitchen paper. Cut into 1cm/½in slices.

**4** Make the teriyaki sauce. Mix the soy sauce, sake or sherry, mirin and sugar together, then heat the mixture in the wok.

**5** Toss in the noodles and stir to coat them in the sauce. Heat for 1–2 minutes, then add the tofu and asparagus and toss lightly to mix. Spoon into warmed serving bowls. Sprinkle the spring onions and carrot batons on top, and sprinkle with the chilli flakes and sesame seeds. Serve immediately.

# PASTA WITH CHEESE & NUTS

Nothing could be simpler or more delicious than the classic combination of pasta and cheese – whether baked in the oven, or served as an elegant dinner-party dish with a rich and creamy sauce. Italian cheeses are world famous and the mouthwatering recipes in this chapter include many of the greatest – Gorgonzola, dolcelatte, ricotta, mozzarella, mascarpone, Pecorino and, of course, Parmesan – each with its own distinctive flavour and texture. Other cheeses, from Greek feta to English Cheddar, also contribute to the wonderful variety of pasta dishes. There are classic recipes, such as Fettuccine all'Alfredo, surprising variations on traditional themes, such as a Caribbean Macaroni Cheese Pie, and some fabulous contemporary ideas, such as Lemon & Parmesan Capellini with Herb Bread. Nuts play an important part in the vegetarian diet and the delicious pasta sauces in this chapter will prove irresistible. Combined with cheese or vegetables, they provide texture and a subtle flavour or they can take a starring role, as in Pasta with Nut & Cream Sauce. Whether you want a warming and hearty dish for a winter supper or an easy, light summer lunch, you are sure to find it here.

## Creamy Pasta with Parmesan Curls

Several perfectly formed curls of Parmesan give a plate of creamy pasta a lift.

**Serves 4–6**
250g/9oz/2¼ cups
   dried campanelle
250g/9oz tub mascarpone cheese
200ml/7fl oz/scant 1 cup
   crème fraîche

75g/3oz/1 cup freshly grated
   Parmesan cheese
115g/4oz/2 cups sun-dried tomatoes
   in oil, drained and thinly sliced
salt and freshly ground
   black pepper

**To garnish**
1 piece of Parmesan cheese,
   about 175g/6oz

**1** Unless you are an old hand at making Parmesan curls, do this first, before cooking the pasta. Holding a swivel-blade vegetable peeler at a 45° angle, draw it steadily across the block of Parmesan cheese to form a curl. Make several curls, depending on the number of guests being served.

**2** Bring a large pan of lightly salted water to the boil and cook the pasta until it is *al dente*.

**3** Meanwhile, put the mascarpone and crème fraîche in a second pan and heat gently until the mascarpone has melted. Add the Parmesan and sun-dried tomatoes and cook over a low heat for 5 minutes. Season with plenty of black pepper and a little salt.

**4** Drain the pasta, return it to the clean pan and pour the sauce over. Toss to mix thoroughly. Serve immediately on warmed individual plates, adding a few Parmesan curls to garnish each portion.

## Fettuccine all'Alfredo

A classic dish from Rome, Fettuccine all'Alfredo is simply pasta tossed with cream, butter and freshly grated Parmesan cheese. It is incredibly quick and simple, perfect for a midweek supper.

**Serves 4**
450g/1lb dried fettuccine
25g/1oz/2 tbsp butter

200ml/7fl oz/scant 1 cup
   double (heavy) cream
50g/2oz/⅔ cup freshly grated
   Parmesan cheese, plus extra
   to serve
freshly grated nutmeg
salt and freshly ground
   black pepper
fresh dill sprigs or chopped fresh
   flat leaf parsley to garnish

**1** Bring a large pan of lightly salted water to the boil and cook the pasta. Allow slightly less time than usual; it should be almost *al dente*, but still slightly firm.

**2** Meanwhile, melt the butter with 150ml/¼ pint/⅔ cup of the cream in a heavy pan. Bring to the boil, then lower the heat and simmer for 1 minute, until slightly thickened. Leave over the lowest possible heat.

**3** Drain the pasta very well and add it to the cream sauce. Keeping the heat low, toss the pasta in the sauce.

**4** Add the remaining cream with the Parmesan and season with salt and pepper to taste. Grate in a little nutmeg. Toss until well coated and heated through. Serve immediately, garnished with dill or parsley and with extra freshly grated Parmesan.

### Cook's Tip
*While fettuccine is traditional, this sauce also goes well with tagliatelle. Pasta shapes, such as penne, rigatoni or farfalle, are also suitable.*

### Cook's Tip
*Mascarpone is a very rich cheese, containing 90 per cent fat. A lighter version, called fiorello light, is now being made. While this is suitable for the health-conscious on a low-fat diet, it is not so delicious as the genuine article.*

# Spaghetti with Feta

We tend to think of pasta as being essentially Italian, but Greeks love it too, especially with feta and tomatoes.

**Serves 2–3**
115g/4oz dried spaghetti
30ml/2 tbsp extra virgin olive oil
1 garlic clove
8 cherry tomatoes, halved
a little freshly grated nutmeg
75g/3oz feta cheese, crumbled
15ml/1 tbsp chopped fresh basil
a few black olives, to serve

**1** Bring a large pan of lightly salted water to the boil and cook the pasta until it is *al dente*. Drain it in a colander.

**2** Heat the olive oil in the clean pan. Add the whole garlic clove and cook it over a low heat for 1–2 minutes. Add the tomatoes, increase the heat and fry them for 1 minute, then remove the garlic and discard.

**3** Toss in the spaghetti, season with the nutmeg, salt and pepper to taste, then stir in the crumbled feta and basil. Toss over the heat to warm the pasta through. Serve in warmed bowls, topped with olives.

**Variation**
*Substitute small pasta shapes for the spaghetti or break the long strands into smaller pieces. Omit the cherry tomatoes. Cut and reserve the tops off four to six beefsteak tomatoes and scoop out the flesh with a teaspoon, leaving the "shell" intact. Place the tomato "shells" upside down on kitchen paper to drain for 20 minutes. Cook the tomato flesh in the garlic-flavoured oil and combine with the other ingredients, including the olives, as described in the recipe. Pile the tossed pasta into the tomato "shells", replace the tops and arrange in an ovenproof dish. Drizzle with a little olive oil and bake in a preheated oven at 190°C/375°F/Gas 5 for 25–30 minutes. In traditional Greek style, serve warm, rather than hot.*

# Tagliatelle with Gorgonzola Sauce

Some dishes are destined to become firm favourites. Without question, this one falls into that category.

**Serves 4**
25g/1oz/2 tbsp butter, plus extra for tossing the pasta
225g/8oz Gorgonzola cheese

150ml/¼ pint/⅔ cup double (heavy) cream
5ml/1 tsp cornflour (cornstarch)
30ml/2 tbsp dry vermouth
15ml/1 tbsp chopped fresh sage
450g/1lb fresh or dried tagliatelle
salt

**1** Melt the butter in a heavy pan. Stir in 175g/6oz of the crumbled Gorgonzola and about one-third of the cream. Stir constantly over a very gentle heat for 2–3 minutes until the cheese has melted.

**2** Mix the cornflour to a paste with the vermouth and add this to the pan with the remaining cream. Whisk over the heat until smooth, then stir in the sage. Keep warm over the lowest possible heat, whisking occasionally.

**3** Bring a large pan of lightly salted water to the boil and cook the pasta until it is *al dente*.

**4** Drain the pasta, return it to the pan and toss with a knob (pat) of butter. Divide among four warmed bowls, top with the sauce and sprinkle over the remaining cheese and serve.

**Cook's Tip**
*When buying Gorgonzola, avoid cheese that is hard in texture or sour smelling.*

**Variation**
*Substitute crumbled Stilton for the Gorgonzola and white port for the vermouth.*

# Penne with Aubergines & Goat's Cheese

Substantial and richly flavoured, this makes a good choice for a winter supper.

**Serves 6**
45ml/3 tbsp olive oil
15g/ ½oz/1 tbsp butter
2 aubergines (eggplants), about 275g/10oz each, cubed
1 garlic clove, chopped
500ml/17fl oz/generous 2 cups passata (bottled strained tomatoes)
15ml/1 tbsp tomato purée (paste)
350g/12oz/3 cups dried penne
115g/4oz firm goat's cheese, cubed
45ml/3 tbsp shredded fresh basil
salt and freshly ground black pepper

**1** Heat half the olive oil and butter in a large, heavy pan. Add the aubergine cubes and fry, stirring frequently, until just golden on all sides, adding more oil and butter if needed.

**2** Stir in the garlic, passata and tomato purée. Bring to the boil, then lower the heat and simmer for 15–20 minutes, until thickened. Season generously.

**3** Bring a large pan of lightly salted water to the boil and cook the pasta until it is *al dente*. Drain well and tip into a warmed serving bowl.

**4** Add the aubergine sauce, goat's cheese and basil to the pasta and toss well. Serve immediately.

**Cook's Tip**
*Montrachet would be a good choice of cheese for this dish. It has a mild, creamy flavour. Made in Burgundy in France, it is ripened for only a few days, wrapped in vine leaves or chestnut leaves. It is usually sold still wrapped in the leaves.*

# Penne with Aubergines & Mint Pesto

This splendid variation on the classic Italian pesto uses fresh mint rather than basil.

**Serves 4**
2 large aubergines (eggplants), about 275g/10oz each
450g/1lb/4 cups dried penne
50g/2oz/ ½ cup walnut halves
salt and freshly ground black pepper

**For the pesto**
25g/1oz/1 cup fresh mint leaves
15g/ ½ oz/ ½ cup flat leaf parsley
40g/1½oz/⅓ cup walnuts
40g/1½oz/ ½ cup freshly grated Parmesan cheese
2 garlic cloves
90ml/6 tbsp olive oil

**1** Cut the aubergines lengthways into 1cm/ ½in slices, then cut the slices again crossways to give short strips.

**2** Layer the aubergine strips in a colander with salt and leave to stand for 30 minutes over a plate to catch any juices. Rinse off the excess salt under cold water and drain.

**3** Make the pesto. Place the mint, parsley, walnuts, Parmesan and garlic in a food processor and blend until smooth. With the motor running, gradually add the oil through the feeder tube in a thin, continuous stream until the mixture amalgamates. Season with salt and pepper to taste.

**4** Bring a large pan of lightly salted water to the boil and cook the penne for 8 minutes. Add the aubergine strips and cook for 3 minutes more.

**5** Drain the pasta and aubergine strips and return the mixture to the clean pan. Add the pesto and walnut halves and toss until combined. Serve immediately.

**Cook's Tip**
*Choose aubergines (eggplants) with glossy, unblemished skins. They should feel firm and heavy for their size.*

# Lemon & Parmesan Capellini with Herb Bread

Cream thickened with Parmesan cheese and flavoured with lemon rind makes a superb and unusual sauce for pasta.

**Serves 2**

½ Granary (whole-
  wheat) baguette
50g/2oz/¼ cup butter, softened
1 garlic clove, crushed
30ml/2 tbsp chopped fresh herbs
225g/8oz fresh or dried capellini
250ml/8fl oz/1 cup single
  (light) cream
75g/3oz/1 cup freshly grated
  Parmesan cheese
finely grated rind of 1 lemon
salt and freshly ground
  black pepper
chopped fresh parsley and grated
  lemon rind (optional), to garnish

**1** Preheat the oven to 200°C/400°F/Gas 6. Cut the baguette into thick slices.

**2** Put the butter in a bowl and beat in the garlic and herbs. Spread thickly over each slice of bread.

**3** Reassemble the baguette. Wrap in foil, support on a baking sheet and bake for 10 minutes.

**4** Meanwhile, bring a large pan of lightly salted water to the boil and cook the pasta until it is *al dente*.

**5** Pour the cream into another pan and bring to the boil. Stir in the Parmesan and lemon rind. The sauce should thicken in about 30 seconds.

**6** Drain the pasta, return it to the clean pan and toss with the sauce. Season to taste and sprinkle with parsley and grated lemon rind, if liked. Serve immediately with the hot herb bread.

> **Cook's Tip**
> *It is best to buy unwaxed lemons if the rind is to be grated.*

# Penne with Fennel Concassé & Blue Cheese

The aniseed flavour of the fennel makes it the perfect partner for pasta in a rich tomato sauce, especially when topped with tasty blue cheese.

**Serves 2**

1 fennel bulb
30ml/2 tbsp extra virgin olive oil
1 shallot, finely chopped
225g/8oz/2 cups dried penne or
  other pasta shapes
300ml/½ pint/1¼ cups passata
  (strained bottled tomatoes)
pinch of granulated sugar
5ml/1 tsp chopped fresh oregano
115g/4oz blue cheese
salt and freshly ground
  black pepper

**1** Cut the fennel bulb in half. Cut away the hard core and root. Slice the fennel thinly, then cut the slices into strips.

**2** Heat the oil in a small pan. Add the fennel and shallot, and cook for 2–3 minutes over a high heat, stirring occasionally.

**3** Meanwhile, bring a large pan of lightly salted water to the boil and cook the pasta until it is *al dente*.

**4** Add the passata, sugar and oregano to the fennel mixture. Cover the pan and simmer gently over a low heat for about 10–12 minutes, until the fennel is tender. Season with salt and pepper to taste.

**5** Drain the pasta and return it to the clean pan. Toss with the sauce. Serve immediately in warmed bowls, with the blue cheese crumbled over the top.

> **Cook's Tip**
> *For a mild flavour, choose a cheese such as dolcelatte or mycella. If you prefer a stronger taste, use Fourme d'Ambert, Bavarian blue or Stilton.*

# Castiglioni with Parmesan Sauce

This is an extremely quick and simple sauce, perfect for anyone in a hurry.

**Serves 4**
450g/1lb/4 cups dried castiglioni
50g/2oz/¼ cup butter
300ml/½ pint/1¼ cups
  double (heavy) cream
175g/6oz/2 cups freshly grated
  Parmesan cheese
30ml/2 tbsp pine nuts, toasted
salt and freshly ground
  black pepper
finely shredded fresh flat leaf
  parsley, to garnish

**1** Bring a large pan of lightly salted water to the boil and cook the pasta until it is *al dente*.

**2** Meanwhile, heat the butter and cream in a pan and stir in half the Parmesan. Heat gently, stirring occasionally, until the Parmesan has melted. Keep the sauce warm.

**3** Drain the pasta and tip it into a warmed serving bowl. Add the remaining Parmesan, season, if needed, and toss until coated. Pour over the sauce and toss again. Sprinkle on the pine nuts and serve immediately, garnished with parsley.

### Cook's Tip
*Double (heavy) cream does not usually curdle when heated, unless there are other very acid ingredients present, such as lemon juice. It can even be boiled without problems. However, it should always be heated gently to avoid the possibility of curdling. Lower fat dairy products, such as single (light) cream, smetana and yogurt, are more likely to curdle and are not, therefore, suitable substitutes.*

### Variation
*If you are unable to find castiglioni – round pasta shapes with scalloped edges – you could use conchiglie instead.*

# Penne with Courgettes & Goat's Cheese

The mild, almost buttery flavour of courgettes is enlivened by the addition of sharp goat's cheese.

**Serves 4**
350g/12oz/3 cups dried penne
60ml/4 tbsp olive oil
2 garlic cloves, chopped
2 large courgettes
  (zucchini), sliced
225g/8oz goat's cheese with
  herbs, diced
30ml/2 tbsp chopped fresh
  oregano, plus oregano sprigs
  to garnish
salt and freshly ground
  black pepper

**1** Bring a large pan of lightly salted water to the boil and cook the pasta until it is *al dente*.

**2** Meanwhile, heat the oil in a large, heavy frying pan. Add the garlic and courgettes, and cook over a gentle heat, stirring occasionally, for 10 minutes.

**3** Add the goat's cheese and chopped oregano and toss over the heat for 1 minute, until heated through.

**4** Drain the pasta thoroughly and return it to the clean pan. Add the courgette mixture and toss well. Season to taste with salt and pepper. Serve in warmed bowls, garnished with the oregano sprigs.

### Variations
• *Diced feta cheese, with its sharp, salty taste, is a good alternative to goat's cheese.*
• *Use smoked, rather than herb-flavoured, goat's cheese.*
• *Substitute 175g/6oz shelled broad (fava) beans for the courgettes (zucchini). Cook them in 175ml/6fl oz/¾ cup Vegetable Stock, then stir them briefly with the garlic in step 2.*
• *Substitute two medium carrots for one of the courgettes. Slice and cook with the courgette, as above.*

# Macaroni & Blue Cheese

This comforting dish is ideal for serving on a chilly evening, or after Christmas, when you may well have the remains of a whole Stilton.

**Serves 6**
butter, for greasing
450g/1lb/4 cups dried short-
    cut macaroni
50g/2oz/ 1/4 cup butter
75g/3oz/ 2/3 cup plain (all-
    purpose) flour
1.2 litres/2 pints/5 cups hot milk
225g/8oz Stilton
    cheese, crumbled
salt and freshly ground
    black pepper

**1** Preheat the oven to 180°C/350°F/Gas 4. Grease a shallow 33 x 23cm/13 x 9in ovenproof dish.

**2** Bring a large pan of lightly salted water to the boil and cook the macaroni until al dente. Drain the macaroni and rinse under cold running water. Drain well again, place in a large bowl and set aside.

**3** Melt the butter in a heavy pan, add the flour and cook over a low heat for 1–2 minutes, stirring constantly. Gradually add the hot milk, whisking constantly until the sauce boils and thickens. Season with salt and pepper to taste.

**4** Stir the sauce into the macaroni. Add three-quarters of the crumbled Stilton and stir well. Transfer the macaroni mixture to the prepared dish and spread evenly.

**5** Sprinkle the remaining cheese evenly over the surface. Bake for about 25 minutes, until the macaroni is bubbling hot. Brown the surface under a hot grill (broiler), if you like.

# Macaroni Cheese with Winter Vegetables

Leeks and celeriac add extra flavour to an ever-popular supper dish.

**Serves 4**
225g/8oz/2 cups dried short-
    cut macaroni
50g/2oz/ 1/4 cup butter
2 leeks, chopped
1 small celeriac root, diced
75ml/5 tbsp plain (all-
    purpose) flour
750ml/1 1/4 pints/3 cups milk
200g/7oz/scant 2 cups grated
    mature (sharp) Cheddar cheese
45ml/3 tbsp fresh
    white breadcrumbs
salt and freshly ground
    black pepper

**1** Preheat the oven to 200°C/400°F/Gas 6. Bring a large pan of lightly salted water to the boil and cook the macaroni until it is al dente.

**2** Meanwhile, melt the butter in a separate pan, add the leeks and celeriac and cook over a medium heat, stirring occasionally, for 4 minutes.

**3** Stir in the flour, and cook, stirring constantly, for 1 minute. Gradually add the milk, stirring constantly until the sauce boils and thickens.

**4** Remove the sauce from the heat. Drain the macaroni well and add it to the sauce, with most of the cheese. Season to taste. Pour the macaroni mixture into a greased ovenproof dish. Mix the breadcrumbs with the remaining cheese, then sprinkle the mixture over the dish. Bake for 20–25 minutes, until the topping is bubbling and golden.

**Cook's Tip**
*Heat the milk before you make the sauce, if you like. It will be absorbed more easily by the flour mixture and the sauce will be less likely to form lumps.*

# Macaroni Soufflé

This is generally a great favourite with children, and is rather like a light and fluffy macaroni cheese.

**Serves 3–4**
75g/3oz/ ³/₄ cup dried short-
   cut macaroni
75g/3oz/6 tbsp butter
45ml/3 tbsp dried breadcrumbs
5ml/1 tsp ground paprika
40g/1 ¹/₂ oz/ ¹/₃ cup plain (all-
   purpose) flour
300ml/ ¹/₂ pint/1 ¹/₄ cups milk
75g/3oz/ ³/₄ cup grated Cheddar
   or Gruyère cheese
50g/2oz/ ²/₃ cup freshly grated
   Parmesan cheese
3 eggs, separated
salt and freshly ground
   black pepper

**1** Preheat the oven to 150°C/300°F/Gas 2. Bring a pan of lightly salted water to the boil and cook the macaroni until *al dente*.

**2** Melt the butter in a pan. Use a little of it to coat the insides of a 1.2 litre/2 pint/5 cup soufflé dish, then coat evenly with the breadcrumbs, shaking out any excess.

**3** Heat the butter remaining in the pan and stir in the paprika and flour. Cook for 1 minute, stirring constantly. Gradually add the milk, stirring until the sauce boils and thickens. Add the grated cheeses, stirring until melted, then season well.

**4** Remove the pan from the heat, cool slightly, then beat in the egg yolks. Whisk the egg whites until they form soft peaks and spoon one-quarter into the sauce mixture, beating it gently.

**5** Using a large metal spoon, carefully fold in the rest of the egg whites. Gently fold in the macaroni. Transfer the mixture to the prepared soufflé dish. Bake in the centre of the oven for about 40–45 minutes, until the soufflé has risen and is golden brown.

> **Cook's Tip**
> *Make sure you serve this as soon as it is cooked or it will sink dramatically. The middle should wobble very slightly.*

# Macaroni Cheese Pie

Macaroni cheese is incredibly popular in the Caribbean and appears in numerous guises.

**Serves 4**
225g/8oz/2 cups dried short-
   cut macaroni
40g/1 ¹/₂oz/3 tbsp butter, plus
   extra for greasing
45ml/3 tbsp plain (all-
   purpose) flour
450ml/ ³/₄ pint/scant 2 cups milk
5ml/1 tsp mild prepared mustard
2.5ml/ ¹/₂ tsp ground cinnamon
175g/6oz/1 ¹/₂ cups grated mature
   (sharp) Cheddar cheese
1 egg, beaten
4 spring onions (scallions),
   finely chopped
40g/1 ¹/₂ oz/3 tbsp canned
   chopped tomatoes
115g/4oz/ ²/₃ cup fresh
   or drained canned
   sweetcorn kernels
salt and freshly ground
   black pepper
chopped fresh parsley, to garnish

**1** Preheat the oven to 180°C/350°F/Gas 4. Bring a large pan of lightly salted water to the boil and cook the macaroni until *al dente*. Rinse under cold water and drain.

**2** Melt 25g/1oz/2 tbsp of the butter in a pan and stir in the flour. Cook for 1–2 minutes, stirring. Gradually add the milk, whisking constantly until the sauce boils and thickens.

**3** Stir in the mustard, cinnamon and two-thirds of the cheese. Cook gently, stirring frequently, until the cheese has melted, then remove from the heat and whisk in the egg. Set aside.

**4** Melt the remaining butter in a small frying pan and cook the spring onions, chopped tomatoes and sweetcorn over a gentle heat for 5–10 minutes. Season to taste.

**5** Tip half the cooked macaroni into a greased ovenproof dish. Pour over half the cheese sauce and mix well, then spoon the tomato and sweetcorn mixture over the macaroni. Stir the remaining macaroni into the remaining cheese sauce, then spread this carefully over the tomato and sweetcorn mixture. Top with the rest of the cheese. Bake for 45 minutes, or until the top is golden and bubbling. Garnish with the parsley.

# Stuffed Conchiglione

This makes an excellent vegetarian main course, but would also be a good choice for a dinner-party appetizer.

**Serves 4**

20 dried conchiglione
25g/1oz/2 tbsp butter
1 small onion, finely chopped
275g/10oz fresh spinach leaves, trimmed, washed and shredded
1 garlic clove, crushed
1 sachet of saffron powder
freshly grated nutmeg
250g/9oz/1½ cups ricotta cheese
1 egg
50g/2oz/⅔ cup freshly grated Parmesan cheese
salt and freshly ground black pepper

**For the sauce**

60ml/4 tbsp olive oil
1 onion, chopped
1 celery stick, chopped
1 carrot, finely chopped
1 garlic clove, sliced
4–5 fresh basil leaves
2 x 400g/14oz cans chopped tomatoes
15ml/1 tbsp tomato purée (paste)
90ml/6 tbsp red wine
300ml/½ pint/1 cup Vegetable Stock
105ml/7 tbsp double (heavy) cream

**1** Bring a large pan of lightly salted water to the boil and cook the pasta shells for 10 minutes. Drain the shells, return them to the pan and cover with cold water.

**2** Make the sauce. Heat the oil in a heavy pan. Add the onion, celery, carrot and garlic, and fry over a medium heat, stirring occasionally, for 10 minutes, until soft.

**3** Add the basil, tomatoes, tomato purée and red wine, bring to the boil, then lower the heat and simmer for 45 minutes, until thick and flavoursome.

**4** Meanwhile, melt the butter in a pan. Add the onion and cook gently, stirring occasionally, for 10 minutes, until softened.

**5** Add the spinach, garlic and saffron, then grate in plenty of nutmeg and stir in salt and pepper to taste. Cook, stirring frequently, for 5–8 minutes, until the spinach is tender.

**6** If the mixture is watery, increase the heat to drive off any excess liquid. Then tip it into a bowl and beat in the ricotta and egg. Preheat the oven to 190°C/375°F/Gas 5.

**7** Purée the tomato sauce in a food processor, then make it up to 750ml/1¼ pints/3 cups with the stock. Stir in the cream.

**8** Spread about half the sauce over the bases of four individual gratin dishes. Drain the pasta shells and fill them with the spinach mixture, using a teaspoon. Arrange five shells in the centre of each dish, spoon the remaining sauce over, then cover with the Parmesan. Bake for 10–12 minutes. Leave to stand for 5 minutes before serving.

# Pasta Pie

This is an excellent supper dish and children absolutely love it.

**Serves 4**

30ml/2 tbsp olive oil
1 small onion, finely chopped
400g/14oz can chopped tomatoes
15ml/1 tbsp sun-dried tomato purée (paste)
5ml/1 tsp dried mixed herbs
5ml/1 tsp dried oregano or basil
5ml/1 tsp granulated sugar
175g/6oz/1½ cups dried conchiglie

30ml/2 tbsp freshly grated Parmesan cheese
30ml/2 tbsp dried breadcrumbs
salt and freshly ground black pepper

**For the cheese sauce**

25g/1oz/2 tbsp butter
25g/1oz/¼ cup plain (all-purpose) flour
600ml/1 pint/2½ cups milk
1 egg
50g/2oz/⅔ cup freshly grated Parmesan cheese

**1** Heat the oil in a large pan and cook the onion until softened. Stir in the tomatoes. Fill the empty can with water and pour it into the pan, then stir in the tomato purée, herbs and sugar.

**2** Season to taste and bring to the boil, stirring. Cover the pan, lower the heat and simmer, stirring occasionally, for 15 minutes.

**3** Preheat the oven to 190°C/375°F/Gas 5. Bring a pan of lightly salted water to the boil and cook the pasta until it is *al dente*.

**4** Meanwhile, make the cheese sauce. Melt the butter in a pan, add the flour and cook, stirring, for 1 minute. Gradually add the milk, stirring constantly until the sauce boils and thickens.

**5** Drain the pasta and tip it into an ovenproof dish. Stir in the tomato sauce. Stir the cheese into the white sauce, beat in the egg, then pour the sauce over the pasta mixture.

**6** Level the surface, sprinkle it with grated Parmesan and breadcrumbs, and bake for 15–20 minutes, or until the topping is golden brown and the cheese is bubbling. Allow to stand for about 10 minutes before serving.

# Tortellini with Cream, Butter & Cheese

This is a wonderfully self-indulgent but extremely quick alternative to macaroni cheese.

**Serves 4–6**
450g/1lb/4 cups fresh tortellini
50g/2oz/¼ cup butter, plus extra for greasing
300ml/½ pint/1¼ cups double (heavy) cream
115g/4oz piece of fresh Parmesan cheese
freshly grated nutmeg
salt and freshly ground black pepper
fresh oregano sprigs, to garnish

**1** Bring a large pan of lightly salted water to the boil and cook the tortellini until al dente.

**2** Meanwhile, melt the butter in a heavy pan over a low heat and stir in the cream. Bring to the boil and cook for about 2–3 minutes, until slightly thickened.

**3** Grate the Parmesan cheese and stir three-quarters of it into the sauce until melted. Season to taste with salt, pepper and nutmeg. Preheat the grill (broiler).

**4** Drain the pasta well and spoon it into a buttered flameproof serving dish. Pour over the sauce, sprinkle over the remaining cheese and place under the grill until brown and bubbling. Serve immediately, garnished with oregano.

> **Variations**
> • Add 15ml/1 tbsp finely chopped fresh oregano or 30ml/2 tbsp finely chopped fresh parsley to the sauce and omit the grated nutmeg.
> • Use mature Gouda or Edam instead of Parmesan.
> • Substitute Manchego for the Parmesan and stir 15–30ml/1–2 tbsp chopped almonds into the sauce before pouring it over the pasta.

# Baked Tortellini with Three Cheeses

Serve this delectable dish straight from the oven while the cheese is still runny.

**Serves 4–6**
450g/1lb/4 cups fresh tortellini
350g/12oz/1½ cups ricotta cheese
2 eggs, beaten
25g/1oz/2 tbsp butter
25g/1oz/1 cup fresh basil leaves
115g/4oz smoked mozzarella cheese, grated
60ml/4 tbsp freshly grated Parmesan cheese
salt and freshly ground black pepper

**1** Preheat the oven to 190°C/375°F/Gas 5. Bring a large pan of lightly salted water to the boil and cook the tortellini until they are al dente.

**2** Mash the ricotta in a large bowl with a fork. Beat in the eggs and season well with salt and pepper.

**3** Use the butter to grease an ovenproof dish. Spoon in half the tortellini, pour over half the ricotta mixture and cover with half the basil leaves.

**4** Cover with the smoked mozzarella and most of the remaining basil, reserving one to two sprigs for the garnish. Top with the rest of the tortellini and spread over the remaining ricotta and egg mixture.

**5** Sprinkle evenly with the Parmesan cheese. Transfer to the oven and bake for 35–45 minutes, or until golden brown and bubbling. Decorate with the reserved basil and serve.

> **Cook's Tip**
> Fresh tortellini with a huge variety of fillings are widely available from supermarkets and delicatessens. A three-cheese, sun-dried tomato or ricotta and spinach filling would go very well in this dish. Plain, spinach-flavoured and tomato-flavoured tortellini are all suitable. Other filled pasta, such as agnolotti or cappelletti, could also be used.

# Butter Bean & Pesto Pasta

Good quality, ready-made pesto is a very useful substitute for home-made. Pesto forms the basis of several very tasty sauces, and it is especially delicious with butter beans.

**Serves 4**
225g/8oz/2 cups dried
   pasta shapes, preferably
   mixed colours
400g/14oz can butter (lima)
   beans, drained

45ml/3 tbsp pesto
150ml/ ¼ pint/ ⅔ cup
   single (light) cream
30ml/2 tbsp extra virgin olive oil
freshly grated nutmeg

**To serve**
45ml/3 tbsp pine nuts
sprigs of fresh basil
freshly grated Parmesan
   cheese (optional)

**1** Bring a large pan of lightly salted water to the boil and cook the pasta until it is *al dente*.

**2** Meanwhile, put the beans in a pan, and stir in the pesto and cream. Heat gently, stirring occasionally, until the mixture simmers. Stir in 15–30ml/1–2 tbsp of the pasta cooking water to thin the sauce if necessary.

**3** Drain the pasta and return it to the clean pan. Toss with the olive oil. Grate in a little nutmeg, then add the bean mixture and toss until well mixed.

**4** Serve in warmed bowls, topped with the pine nuts and garnished with the basil sprigs. Offer grated Parmesan cheese for sprinkling, if you like.

> **Variations**
> • *Other beans may be used instead of the butter (lima) beans. Borlotti or cannellini would work well.*
> • *For a change of flavour, use red pesto, made with sun-dried tomatoes, rather than traditional basil pesto.*

# Fusilli with Lentil & Cheese Sauce

Lentils make a good sauce for pasta, with plenty of body and flavour. This is a delicious and filling supper dish, ideal for winter nights.

**Serves 4**
75g/2½ oz/ ⅓ cup green lentils
15ml/1 tbsp olive oil
1 onion, chopped
1 garlic clove, chopped
1 carrot, cut into thin batons

350g/12oz/3 cups dried fusilli
15ml/1 tbsp tomato
   purée (paste)
15ml/1 tbsp chopped
   fresh oregano
150ml/ ¼ pint/ ⅔ cup
   Vegetable Stock
225g/8oz/2 cups grated Cheddar
   cheese, plus extra to serve
salt and freshly ground
   black pepper

**1** Pick over the lentils. Put them in a pan with cold water to cover generously. Bring to the boil and cook for 25–30 minutes, until tender. Drain and set aside.

**2** Heat the oil in a large frying pan, and fry the onion and garlic over a medium heat, stirring occasionally, for 3 minutes. Add the carrot and cook for a further 5 minutes.

**3** Bring a pan of lightly salted water to the boil and cook the pasta until it is *al dente*.

**4** Meanwhile, stir the lentils, tomato purée and oregano into the vegetable mixture, cover and cook for 2 minutes. Stir in the stock, and season with salt and pepper to taste. Cover and simmer for 10 minutes. Stir in the cheese.

**5** Drain the pasta thoroughly and stir it into the sauce to coat. Serve in warmed bowls, and hand round plenty of extra grated cheese separately.

> **Cook's Tip**
> *Many vegetarians swear that adding a little yeast extract to lentils brings out their flavour. Try it and see.*

# Farfalle with Fennel & Walnut Sauce

A scrumptious blend of walnuts and crisp steamed fennel, this always goes down well.

**Serves 4**
75g/3oz/ ³⁄₄ cup walnuts
1 garlic clove
25g/1oz/1 cup fresh flat leaf
  parsley, stalks removed
115g/4oz/ ¹⁄₂ cup ricotta cheese
450g/1lb dried farfalle
450g/1lb fennel bulbs, trimmed
  and thinly sliced
chopped walnuts, to garnish

**1** Place the walnuts, garlic and parsley in a food processor. Pulse until roughly chopped. Transfer to a bowl and stir in the ricotta.

**2** Bring a large pan of lightly salted water to the boil and cook the pasta until it is *al dente*.

**3** Meanwhile, steam the fennel for 4–5 minutes, until just tender but still crisp.

**4** Drain the pasta, return it to the clean pan and add the walnut mixture and the fennel. Toss well and sprinkle with the extra chopped walnuts. Serve immediately.

---

**Cook's Tip**
*When preparing the fennel, cut off and reserve the feathery fronds. Use them as an extra garnish, if you like.*

---

**Variation**
*As they have a special affinity with fennel, you could substitute pistachio nuts for the walnuts.*

---

# Tagliatelle with Olive & Pecan Sauce

This is an unusual sauce that would make this dish a spectacular first course at a dinner party.

**Serves 4–6**
2 thick slices wholemeal (whole-
  wheat) bread
300ml/ ¹⁄₂ pint/1 ¹⁄₄ cups milk
275g/10oz/2 ¹⁄₂ cups pecan nuts
115g/4oz/1 cup pitted
  black olives
1 garlic clove, crushed
50g/2oz/ ²⁄₃ cup freshly grated
  Parmesan cheese
90ml/6 tbsp olive oil, plus extra
  for tossing the pasta
150ml/ ¹⁄₄ pint/ ²⁄₃ cup
  double (heavy) cream
450g/1lb fresh or dried tagliatelle
30ml/2 tbsp chopped
  fresh parsley
salt and freshly ground
  black pepper

**1** Preheat the oven to 190°C/375°F/Gas 5. Cut the crusts off the bread. Put the slices in a shallow bowl and pour over the milk. Leave to soak until all the milk is absorbed.

**2** Spread the pecans on a baking sheet and toast in the oven for 5 minutes. Leave to cool.

**3** Place the soaked bread, pecans, olives, garlic, Parmesan and olive oil in a food processor and blend until smooth. Season to taste with salt and pepper. Add the cream and process briefly again to mix.

**4** Bring a large pan of lightly salted water to the boil and cook the pasta until it is *al dente*. Drain well and toss with a little olive oil. Divide the pasta equally among individual bowls and place a generous spoonful of sauce on each portion. Sprinkle with chopped parsley and serve immediately.

---

**Variation**
*Pecans tend to be rather expensive. For economy, substitute walnut pieces.*

---

# Pasta with Courgette & Walnut Sauce

For the best flavour, use the youngest, freshest courgettes you can find for this tasty dish.

**Serves 4**

65g/2½ oz/5 tbsp butter
1 large Spanish onion, halved and thinly sliced
450g/1lb courgettes (zucchini), very thinly sliced
350g/12oz dried pasta shapes
50g/2oz/ ½ cup walnuts, coarsely chopped
45ml/3 tbsp chopped fresh parsley
30ml/2 tbsp single (light) cream
salt and freshly ground black pepper
freshly grated Parmesan cheese, to serve

**1** Melt the butter in a heavy frying pan. Add the onion, cover and cook gently over a low heat for 5 minutes, then add the sliced courgettes.

**2** Stir well, cover again and continue to cook over a low heat until the vegetables are very soft, stirring occasionally.

**3** Meanwhile, bring a large pan of lightly salted water to the boil and cook the pasta until it is *al dente*.

**4** While the pasta is cooking, add the walnuts, parsley and cream to the courgette mixture and stir well. Season with salt and pepper to taste.

**5** Drain the pasta and return it to the clean pan. Add the courgette sauce and mix well. Serve in warmed bowls, with freshly grated Parmesan to sprinkle on top of each portion.

> **Cook's Tip**
> *The onions and courgettes (zucchini) should not be fried, but "sweated" in the butter. A gentle heat is used and, because there is a lid on the pan, the technique resembles steaming.*

# Penne with Broccoli & Pecans

This sauce is absolutely delicious with pasta and can also be spread on slices of fresh or toasted ciabatta.

**Serves 4**

275g/10oz/2½ cups dried penne
450g/1lb fresh broccoli, cut into equal-size florets
salt

**For the sauce**

50g/2oz/ ½ cup pecan nuts
30ml/2 tbsp fresh brown breadcrumbs
75g/3oz/1½ cups roughly chopped fresh parsley
120ml/4fl oz/ ½ cup extra virgin olive oil
30ml/2 tbsp single (light) cream
salt and freshly ground black pepper

**1** First make the sauce. Place the pecans, breadcrumbs and parsley in a blender or food processor and process for 20 seconds. With the motor running, gradually add the olive oil through the lid or feeder tube to make a slightly textured paste. Add the cream, season with salt and pepper to taste and process briefly to mix.

**2** Bring a large pan of lightly salted water to the boil and cook the pasta until it is *al dente*.

**3** Steam the broccoli florets for about 3 minutes, until they are tender but retain a little crunch.

**4** Drain the pasta, place in a bowl and mix with the broccoli. Spoon on to warmed serving plates and pour the sauce over.

> **Variations**
> *• You can substitute hazelnuts for the pecans. Roast them first by spreading them out on a grill (broiler) pan and placing them under a medium heat until they are golden. Shake the pan from time to time and watch them closely, because they burn readily. Let them cool slightly, then tip them into a clean dishtowel and rub off the skins before using them in the sauce.*
> *• Serve with spirali instead of penne.*

# Pasta with Nut & Cream Sauce

Based on a classic Italian recipe, this has a strong, nutty flavour, and should be accompanied by a salad of dressed leaves.

**Serves 4**

50g/2oz/ ½ cup walnut pieces
50g/2oz/ ½ cup hazelnuts
350g/12oz dried fusilli lunghi
  or spaghetti
25g/1oz/2 tbsp butter
300ml/ ½ pint/1¼ cups
  single (light) cream
50g/2oz/1 cup fresh
  white breadcrumbs
25g/1oz/ ⅓ cup freshly grated
  Parmesan cheese
pinch of freshly grated nutmeg
salt and freshly ground
  black pepper
fresh rosemary sprigs, to garnish

**1** Preheat the grill (broiler). Spread the walnuts and hazelnuts in an even layer in the grill pan and place under a medium heat for about 5 minutes, shaking the pan occasionally, until they are evenly toasted and golden.

**2** Let the nuts cool slightly, tip them into a clean dishtowel and rub off the skins. Chop the nuts roughly and set them aside.

**3** Bring a large pan of lightly salted water to the boil and cook the pasta until it is *al dente*.

**4** Meanwhile, heat the butter and cream in a pan until the butter is melted. Stir in the breadcrumbs and nuts and heat gently, stirring constantly, for 2 minutes, until thickened. Add the Parmesan, nutmeg and seasoning to taste. Stir over a low heat until the cheese has melted.

**5** Drain the pasta thoroughly and tip it into a warmed serving bowl. Add the sauce and toss to coat. Serve immediately, garnished with the fresh rosemary.

---

**Variation**

*Try using different cheeses in the walnut sauce. Gorgonzola or Roquefort could be used instead of Parmesan, or even Stilton.*

---

# Macaroni with Hazelnut & Coriander Sauce

This is a very simple recipe. The reason it works so well is because the warm, earthy flavour of the nuts is balanced by the exotic taste of the coriander.

**Serves 4**

50g/2oz/ ½ cup hazelnuts
350g/12oz short-cut macaroni
2 garlic cloves, halved
1 bunch fresh coriander (cilantro)
90ml/6 tbsp olive oil
salt and freshly ground
  black pepper
fresh coriander (cilantro) sprigs,
  to garnish

**1** Preheat the grill (broiler). Spread out the hazelnuts in the grill pan and place them under a medium heat, shaking the pan occasionally, for 5 minutes, or until toasted and golden.

**2** Let the hazelnuts cool slightly, then tip them into a clean dishtowel and rub off the skins.

**3** Bring a large pan of lightly salted water to the boil and cook the macaroni until it is *al dente*.

**4** Meanwhile, put the nuts in a food processor and chop them finely, then add the garlic, coriander and 5ml/1 tsp salt. Process until the coriander is chopped, then, with the motor running, gradually add 75ml/5 tbsp of the oil through the feeder tube, until the mixture forms a thick sauce. Season with salt and pepper to taste.

**5** Heat the remaining olive oil in a heavy pan and add the sauce. Fry very gently, stirring constantly, for about 1 minute, until heated through.

**6** Drain the pasta thoroughly and stir it into the sauce. Toss well to coat. Serve immediately, garnished with fresh coriander.

# Paglia e Fieno with Walnuts & Gorgonzola

The nuts and different cheeses make this dish very rich, and it would make an excellent dinner-party appetizer for 6–8 people.

**Serves 4**
275g/10oz dried paglia e fieno
25g/1oz/2 tbsp butter
5ml/1 tsp finely chopped fresh sage
115g/4oz torta di Gorgonzola cheese, diced
45ml/3 tbsp mascarpone cheese
75ml/5 tbsp milk
50g/2oz/ 1/2 cup walnut halves, ground
30ml/2 tbsp freshly ground Parmesan cheese
salt and freshly ground black pepper

**1** Bring a large pan of lightly salted water to the boil and cook the pasta until it is *al dente*.

**2** Meanwhile, melt the butter in a large pan over a low heat, add the sage and stir. Add the Gorgonzola and mascarpone and stir until they start to melt. Stir in the milk.

**3** Sprinkle in the walnuts and Parmesan and add plenty of black pepper. Continue to stir over a low heat until the mixture forms a creamy sauce. Do not allow it to boil or the nuts will taste bitter. Do not cook the sauce for longer than a few minutes or the nuts will discolour it.

**4** Drain the pasta, tip it into a warmed bowl, then add the sauce and toss well. Serve immediately, with more black pepper ground on top.

> **Cook's Tip**
> *Ready-ground nuts are sold in packets in supermarkets, but you will get a better flavour if you buy walnut halves and grind them yourself in a food processor.*

# Pipe with Ricotta, Saffron & Spinach

Serve this fairly rich dish in small quantities. Omit the saffron, with its quite strong flavour, if you like.

**Serves 4–6**
300g/11oz/2¾ cups dried pipe
300–350g/11–12oz fresh spinach leaves
freshly grated nutmeg
250g/9oz/generous 1 cup ricotta cheese
1 small pinch of saffron threads soaked in 60ml/4 tbsp warm water
salt and freshly ground black pepper
freshly grated Pecorino cheese, to serve

**1** Bring a large pan of lightly salted water to the boil and cook the pasta until it is *al dente*.

**2** Meanwhile, wash the spinach and put the leaves in a pan with only the water that clings to the leaves. Season with freshly grated nutmeg and salt and pepper to taste.

**3** Cover the pan and cook over a medium to high heat, shaking the pan occasionally, for 5 minutes, until the spinach is wilted and tender. Tip into a colander, press it to extract as much liquid as possible, then roughly chop it.

**4** Put the ricotta in a large bowl. Strain in the saffron water. Add the spinach, beat well to mix, then add one to two ladlefuls of the pasta cooking water to loosen the mixture. Season to taste with salt and pepper.

**5** Drain the pasta and add it to the ricotta mixture. Toss well. Serve in warmed bowls, sprinkled with Pecorino.

> **Cook's Tip**
> *For the best results, use fresh white ricotta, which is sold by weight in Italian delicatessens.*

# SIMPLY VEGETABLES

Pasta and vegetables must be some of the most versatile ingredients in the world. Put them together and the possibilities are virtually endless. Colourful Mediterranean produce, such as (bell) peppers, tomatoes, aubergines (eggplants) and courgettes (zucchini), have a natural affinity with pasta and this chapter features a really marvellous collection of traditional dishes that almost taste of Italian sunshine. Mushrooms, too, offer an immense variety of flavours, colours and textures. Wild or cultivated, fresh or dried, their distinctive taste makes them irresistible with pasta. Other inspirational recipes are based on vegetables less commonly associated with pasta, but no less delicious. Try ringing the changes with Green Pasta with Avocado Sauce or Pasta with Savoy Cabbage & Gruyère, for example. Whatever the season, this chapter offers the ideal dish for every occasion. Vegetables and noodles are staples in the diets of many Asian countries and, over the centuries, their cooks have developed a repertoire of exciting and attractive dishes to stimulate – and satisfy – the appetite. Fried noodles are a speciality and are the perfect partner for a crisp-tender, stir-fried medley of vegetables served in a subtle, complementary sauce. Often speedy to prepare, usually easy to cook and always delicious, the recipes in this chapter show vegetarian cooking at its best.

# Trenette with Pesto, Green Beans & Potatoes

Potatoes are almost as good with pesto as is pasta, so any recipe that combines all three ingredients is bound to be a winner.

**Serves 4**
about 40 fresh basil leaves
2 garlic cloves, thinly sliced
25ml/1½ tbsp pine nuts
45ml/3 tbsp freshly grated
   Parmesan cheese, plus extra
   to serve
30ml/2 tbsp freshly grated
   Pecorino cheese, plus extra
   to serve
60ml/4 tbsp extra virgin olive oil
2 potatoes, total weight about
   250g/9oz
100g/3½ oz green beans
350g/12oz dried trenette
salt and freshly ground
   black pepper

**1** Put the basil leaves, garlic, pine nuts and cheeses in a blender or food processor and process for about 5 seconds. Add half the olive oil and a pinch of salt and process for 5 seconds more. Stop the machine, remove the lid and scrape down the side of the bowl. Add the remaining olive oil and process for 5–10 seconds.

**2** Peel the potatoes and cut each one in half lengthways. Slice each half crossways into 5mm/¼in thick slices. Trim the beans, then cut them into 2cm/¾in pieces. Bring a large pan of lightly salted water to the boil. Add the potatoes and beans and boil, uncovered, for 5 minutes.

**3** Add the pasta, bring the water back to the boil, stir well, then cook until the pasta is *al dente*.

**4** Meanwhile, put the pesto in a large bowl and thin it with 45–60ml/3–4 tbsp of the water used for cooking the pasta.

**5** Drain the pasta and vegetables, add them to the pesto and toss well. Serve immediately on warmed plates, with extra grated Parmesan and Pecorino handed separately.

# Pasta with Mixed Vegetable Medley

Tossed with freshly cooked pasta, this delicious mixture of tender vegetables is ideal for a fresh and light lunch or supper.

**Serves 4**
2 carrots
1 courgette (zucchini)
75g/3oz green beans
1 small leek
2 ripe Italian plum tomatoes
a handful of fresh flat leaf parsley
25g/1oz/2 tbsp butter
45ml/3 tbsp extra virgin olive oil
2.5ml/½ tsp granulated sugar
115g/4oz/1 cup frozen peas
450g/1lb/4 cups fresh or dried
   penne rigate or other
   pasta shapes
salt and freshly ground
   black pepper

**1** Dice the carrots and courgette finely. Trim the green beans, then cut them into 2cm/¾in lengths. Slice the leek thinly. Peel and dice the tomatoes. Chop the parsley and set it aside.

**2** Melt the butter in the oil in a medium pan and add the prepared leek and carrots. Sprinkle the sugar over and cook, stirring frequently, for about 5 minutes.

**3** Stir in the courgette, green beans, peas and plenty of salt and pepper. Cover and cook gently until the vegetables are tender, stirring occasionally.

**4** Meanwhile, bring a large pan of lightly salted water to the boil. Add the pasta and cook until *al dente*.

**5** Stir the parsley and chopped plum tomatoes into the vegetable mixture and adjust the seasoning. Drain the pasta, return it to the clean pan and add the vegetable mixture. Toss well and serve immediately.

---

**Variations**
*Use fresh peas when they are in season or substitute mangetouts (snow peas) for the frozen peas and baby corn cobs for the green beans.*

# Pasta with Aubergines & Tomato Sauce

This pasta recipe was popular long before roasted vegetables became fashionable. It is delicious.

**Serves 4**

2 medium aubergines (eggplants), about 225g/8oz each, diced
45ml/3 tbsp olive oil
275g/10oz/2½ cups dried macaroni or fusilli
50g/2oz/⅔ cup grated Pecorino cheese

salt and freshly ground black pepper
shredded fresh basil leaves, to garnish

**For the tomato sauce**

30ml/2 tbsp olive oil
1 onion, finely chopped
400g/14oz can chopped tomatoes
10ml/2 tsp balsamic vinegar

**1** Preheat the oven to 220°C/425°F/Gas 7. Make the sauce. Heat the oil in a large pan and fry the onion gently until softened. Add the tomatoes and season. Bring to the boil, lower the heat, cover and simmer for 20 minutes. Stir the sauce and add a little water if it gets too thick. Remove from the heat.

**2** Spread out the diced aubergines in a roasting pan, add the oil and toss to coat. Roast for 20–25 minutes, turning the pieces every 4–5 minutes with a spatula so that they brown evenly.

**3** Bring a large pan of lightly salted water to the boil and cook the pasta until it is *al dente*.

**4** Drain the pasta thoroughly and return it to the clean pan. Reheat the sauce and stir in the vinegar. Add it to the pasta with half the roasted aubergine and half the Pecorino. Toss to mix, then taste for seasoning.

**5** Spoon the mixture into a warmed large serving dish and top with the remaining roasted aubergine. Sprinkle the shredded basil leaves over the top, followed by the remaining grated Pecorino. Serve immediately.

# Spaghetti with Aubergine & Ricotta

Do try to locate ricotta salata for this classic dish. Its slight saltiness is the ideal match for the richness of the aubergine.

**Serves 4–6**

60ml/4 tbsp olive oil
1 garlic clove, coarsely chopped
450g/1lb ripe plum tomatoes, peeled and chopped

vegetable oil for shallow frying
1 large aubergine (eggplant), about 350g/12oz, diced
400g/14oz fresh or dried spaghetti
1 handful fresh basil leaves, shredded
115g/4oz ricotta salata cheese, coarsely grated
salt and freshly ground black pepper

**1** Heat the olive oil in a pan, add the garlic and cook over a low heat, stirring constantly, for 1–2 minutes. Stir in the tomatoes, then season with salt and pepper to taste. Cover and simmer for 20 minutes.

**2** Meanwhile, heat the oil for shallow frying in a frying pan and fry the aubergine cubes, in batches, for 4–5 minutes, until tender and lightly browned. As each batch cooks, remove it with a slotted spoon and drain on kitchen paper.

**3** Bring a large pan of lightly salted water to the boil and cook the pasta until it is *al dente*. Meanwhile, stir the fried aubergine into the tomato sauce and warm through. Taste and adjust the seasoning, if necessary.

**4** Drain the pasta and tip it into a warmed bowl. Add the sauce, with the shredded basil and a generous handful of the grated ricotta salata. Toss well and serve immediately, with the remaining ricotta sprinkled on top.

**Cook's Tip**
*In Italy, this dish is known as spaghetti alla Bellini and is named after the Sicilian composer. It is sometimes also called spaghetti alla Norma, after his opera.*

# Heavenly Tomato Pasta

Delicate angel hair pasta served with a rocket, tomato and lime sauce is a rare treat.

**Serves 4**
450g/1lb very ripe tomatoes, peeled and chopped
1 small bunch of tender, young rocket (arugula) leaves
4 garlic cloves, crushed
grated rind of ½ lime
juice of 2 limes
1.5ml/¼ tsp Tabasco sauce
60ml/4 tbsp olive oil
350g/12oz capellini (angel hair pasta)
salt and freshly ground black pepper
freshly grated Parmesan cheese, to serve

**1** Combine the tomatoes, rocket, garlic, lime rind and juice in a bowl. Stir in the Tabasco sauce and olive oil, then cover and set aside for 20–30 minutes.

**2** Bring a large pan of lightly salted water to the boil and cook the pasta until it is *al dente*.

**3** Drain the pasta and return it to the clean pan. Add the tomato mixture and toss well. Season with salt and pepper to taste. Add Parmesan cheese to taste, toss again and serve in warmed bowls, with extra Parmesan on top, if you like.

**Cook's Tip**
*Tabasco sauce is made from chillies and has a distinctive aroma and hot flavour. The original sauce was made from red chillies, but a green Tabasco, made from jalapeño chillies, is now available. It is slightly milder. There are also many other pepper sauces available.*

**Variation**
*You could substitute young sorrel leaves or baby spinach for the rocket (arugula), and lemon juice and rind for the lime.*

# Sun-dried Tomato & Parmesan Carbonara

Classic carbonara contains prosciutto or bacon. This vegetarian version substitutes sun-dried tomatoes, with excellent results. Serve it with a crisp green salad and plenty of fresh, crusty bread.

**Serves 4**
175g/6oz dried tagliatelle
2 eggs, beaten
150ml/¼ pint/⅔ cup double (heavy) cream
15ml/1 tbsp wholegrain mustard
50g/2oz/½ cup sun-dried tomatoes in olive oil, drained and thinly sliced
50g/2oz/⅔ cup freshly grated Parmesan cheese
12 fresh basil leaves, shredded, plus whole sprigs, to garnish
salt and freshly ground black pepper

**1** Bring a pan of lightly salted water to the boil and cook the pasta until it is *al dente*.

**2** Whisk together the eggs, cream and mustard in a bowl. Add plenty of seasoning and whisk again.

**3** Drain the pasta and return it to the pan. Add the cream mixture, sun-dried tomatoes, Parmesan and basil. Toss over a very low heat for 1 minute, until the mixture thickens slightly.

**4** Adjust the seasoning and serve immediately, garnished with the basil sprigs.

**Cook's Tip**
*You can include additional ingredients, such as lightly fried onion and garlic, fresh or dried mushrooms or black olives, stirring them in with the sun-dried tomatoes in step 3. Whatever extras you include, it is important that the mixture is heated through very quickly so the eggs have no time to scramble.*

# Green Pasta with Avocado Sauce

Avocados make a rich and creamy sauce, which looks very effective on spinach-flavoured tagliatelle.

**Serves 6**
3 ripe tomatoes
2 large ripe avocados
450g/1lb dried spinach-
    flavoured tagliatelle

25g/1oz/2 tbsp butter, plus extra
    for tossing the pasta
1 garlic clove, crushed
350ml/12fl oz/1½ cups
    double (heavy) cream
dash of Tabasco sauce
salt and freshly ground
    black pepper
freshly grated Parmesan cheese
    and sour cream, to serve

**1** Cut the tomatoes in half and remove the cores. Squeeze out the seeds and cut the tomatoes into dice. Set aside.

**2** Cut the avocados in half, take out the stones (pits) and remove the peel. Chop the flesh roughly.

**3** Bring a pan of lightly salted water to the boil and cook the pasta until it is *al dente*.

**4** Meanwhile, melt the butter in a pan and add the garlic. Cook over a low heat for 1 minute, then add the cream and chopped avocados. Increase the heat and cook for 5 minutes, stirring constantly to break up the avocados.

**5** Add the diced tomatoes and season to taste with salt, pepper and a little Tabasco sauce.

**6** Drain the pasta, return it to the clean pan and toss it with a knob (pat) of butter. Divide it among four warmed bowls and spoon over the sauce. Sprinkle with grated Parmesan and serve with sour cream handed separately.

**Variation**
*Sprinkle with chopped chives instead of serving with sour cream if you prefer a less rich dish.*

# Buckwheat Noodles with Cabbage

This is a very unusual pasta dish. The buckwheat noodles used are unique to Valtellina in the Italian Alps, where the dish originated.

**Serves 6**
400g/14oz Savoy cabbage, cut
    into 1cm/½in strips
2 potatoes, cut into 5mm/
    ¼in slices
400g/14oz dried pizzoccheri
    (Italian buckwheat noodles)

75g/3oz/6 tbsp butter
a generous bunch of fresh sage
    leaves, shredded
2 garlic cloves
200g/7oz Fontina cheese, rind
    removed and thinly sliced
30–45ml/2–3 tbsp freshly grated
    Parmesan cheese, plus extra
    to serve
salt

**1** Bring a very large pan of lightly salted water to the boil. Add the cabbage and potatoes and boil for 5 minutes.

**2** Add the pasta, stir well and let the water return to the boil. Lower the heat and simmer for 15 minutes, or until the pasta is *al dente*.

**3** A few minutes before the pasta is ready, melt the butter in a small pan. Add the sage and whole garlic cloves and fry gently until the garlic is golden and sizzling. Lift the garlic out of the pan and discard it. Set the flavoured butter aside.

**4** Drain the pasta and vegetables. Pour a quarter of the mixture into a warmed large bowl and arrange about a third of the Fontina slices on top. Repeat these layers until all the ingredients have been used, then sprinkle with the grated Parmesan. Pour the sage and garlic butter over the top and serve immediately, with extra Parmesan handed separately.

**Cook's Tip**
*Packets of dried pizzoccheri pasta are available from good Italian delicatessens.*

# Tagliatelle with Tomatoes & Courgettes

Courgettes add texture and fresh colour to the tagliatelle in this simple dish.

**Serves 3–4**
225g/8oz wholewheat tagliatelle
30ml/2 tbsp olive oil
1 onion, chopped
2 celery sticks, chopped
1 garlic clove, crushed
2 courgettes (zucchini), sliced
5–6 ripe tomatoes, peeled and chopped
30ml/2 tbsp sun-dried tomato purée (paste)
50g/2oz/½ cup flaked (sliced) almonds, toasted
salt and freshly ground black pepper

**1** Bring a large pan of lightly salted water to the boil, add the pasta and cook until *al dente*.

**2** Meanwhile, heat the olive oil in another pan. Add the onion, celery and garlic, and cook, stirring frequently, over a gentle heat for 3–4 minutes, or until the onions have softened and are lightly browned.

**3** Stir in the courgettes, tomatoes and sun-dried tomato purée. Cook over a low heat, stirring occasionally, for 5 minutes, until the courgettes are crisp-tender, then season with salt and pepper to taste.

**4** Drain the pasta, return it to the clean pan and add the sauce. Toss well. Place in a warmed serving dish and sprinkle the toasted almonds over the top to serve.

> **Variation**
> Use banana (yellow) courgettes (zucchini) for a change, or a mixture of both colours.

# Pasta with Spring Vegetables

Celebrate the arrival of tender, new-season vegetables with this colourful, creamy pasta dish.

**Serves 4**
115g/4oz/scant 1 cup broccoli florets
115g/4oz baby leeks, trimmed
225g/8oz asparagus spears, trimmed
1 small fennel bulb
115g/4oz/1 cup fresh or frozen peas
350g/12oz dried penne
40g/1½ oz/3 tbsp butter
1 shallot, chopped
45ml/3 tbsp chopped fresh mixed herbs, such as parsley, thyme and sage
300ml/½ pint/1¼ cups double (heavy) cream
salt and freshly ground black pepper
freshly grated Parmesan cheese, to serve

**1** Divide the broccoli florets into tiny sprigs. Cut the leeks and asparagus diagonally into 5cm/2in lengths. Trim the fennel bulb and remove any tough outer leaves. Cut it into wedges, leaving the layers attached at the root end so the pieces stay intact.

**2** Cook each vegetable separately, one after the other, in a large pan of lightly salted boiling water until just tender. Remove each batch of vegetables with a slotted spoon and place them in a bowl. Keep hot. (Using the same water each time for cooking the vegetables creates a simple vegetable stock which is perfect for cooking the pasta.)

**3** Bring the water used for cooking the vegetables back to the boil. Add the pasta and cook until *al dente*.

**4** Meanwhile, melt the butter in another pan. Add the shallot and fry over a medium heat, stirring occasionally, until softened, but not browned. Stir in the vegetables, with the herbs and cream. Season to taste with salt and pepper, and cook for a few minutes, until thickened.

**5** Drain the pasta and return it to the clean pan. Add the sauce and toss lightly. Serve in warmed bowls, topped with Parmesan.

# Rigatoni with Winter Tomato Sauce

In winter, when fresh tomatoes are not at their best, this is the sauce the Italians serve with their favourite pasta.

**Serves 6–8**
60ml/4 tbsp olive oil
1 garlic clove, thinly sliced
1 onion, finely chopped
1 carrot, finely chopped
1 celery stick, finely chopped
a few leaves each fresh basil,
   thyme and oregano or
   marjoram, plus extra, to garnish
2 x 400g/14oz cans chopped
   Italian plum tomatoes
15ml/1 tbsp sun-dried
   tomato purée (paste)
5ml/1 tsp granulated sugar
about 90ml/6 tbsp dry red or
   white wine (optional)
350g/12oz/3 cups dried rigatoni
salt and freshly ground
   black pepper
coarsely shaved Parmesan cheese,
   to serve

**1** Heat the olive oil in a large, heavy pan. Add the garlic slices and cook, stirring constantly, over a very low heat for about 1–2 minutes.

**2** Add the onion, carrot, celery and the fresh herbs. Cook over a low heat, stirring frequently, for 5–7 minutes, until the vegetables have softened and are lightly coloured.

**3** Add the canned tomatoes, tomato purée and sugar and then stir in the wine, if using. Season with salt and pepper to taste. Bring to the boil, stirring constantly, then lower the heat so that the mixture is simmering gently. Cook, uncovered, for about 45 minutes, stirring occasionally, until the vegetables are tender and the sauce has thickened.

**4** Bring a large pan of lightly salted water to the boil. Add the pasta and cook until it is *al dente*. Drain it and tip it into a warmed serving bowl.

**5** Pour the sauce over the pasta and toss thoroughly. Serve immediately, with shavings of Parmesan handed separately. Garnish with the extra herbs.

# Fusilli with Tomato & Balsamic Vinegar

The intense, sweet-sour flavour of balsamic vinegar gives a pleasantly gentle kick to a sauce made with canned tomatoes.

**Serves 6–8**
2 x 400g/14oz cans chopped
   Italian plum tomatoes
2 drained sun-dried tomatoes in
   olive oil, thinly sliced
2 garlic cloves, crushed
45ml/3 tbsp olive oil
5ml/1 tsp granulated sugar
350g/12oz/3 cups fresh or
   dried fusilli
45ml/3 tbsp balsamic vinegar
salt and freshly ground
   black pepper
rocket (arugula) salad, country
   bread and coarsely shaved
   Pecorino cheese, to serve

**1** Put the canned tomatoes and sun-dried tomatoes in a medium pan with the garlic, olive oil and sugar. Season with salt and pepper to taste. Bring to the boil over a medium heat, stirring constantly. Lower the heat and simmer gently for about 30 minutes, until reduced.

**2** Meanwhile, bring a large pan of lightly salted water to the boil. Add the pasta and cook until it is *al dente*.

**3** Stir the balsamic vinegar into the tomato sauce. Cook for 1–2 minutes more.

**4** Drain the pasta and return it to the clean pan. Pour the sauce over and toss well. Serve in warmed bowls, with rocket salad and bread. Offer the shaved Pecorino separately.

**Cook's Tip**
*Balsamic vinegar from Modena is expensive, but its price is an indication of its quality. Cheaper imitations have either not been matured for the requisite minimum of 12 years or are made from red wine vinegar that is coloured and flavoured with caramel. Real balsamic vinegar has a mellow and concentrated flavour.*

# Pasta with Savoy Cabbage & Gruyère

This is an inexpensive and simple dish with a surprising texture and flavour. The cabbage retains some crispness and contrasts beautifully with the pasta.

**Serves 4**

25g/1oz/2 tbsp butter, plus extra
  for greasing
350g/12oz fresh or
  dried tagliatelle
1 small Savoy or green cabbage,
  thinly sliced
1 small onion, chopped
15ml/1 tbsp chopped
  fresh parsley
150ml/ ¼ pint/ ²⁄₃ cup
  single (light) cream
50g/2oz/ ½ cup grated Gruyère
  or Cheddar cheese
about 300ml/ ½ pint/1 ¼ cups
  hot Vegetable Stock
salt and freshly ground
  black pepper

**1** Preheat the oven to 180°C/350°F/Gas 4 and grease a large ovenproof dish with butter. Bring a large pan of lightly salted water to the boil and cook the pasta until it is *al dente*.

**2** Meanwhile, place the cabbage in a mixing bowl. Melt the butter in a small frying pan and fry the onion until softened. Add it to the cabbage and mix well.

**3** Drain the pasta and add it to the cabbage mixture, with the parsley. Mix well and then pour into the prepared dish.

**4** Beat together the single cream and grated Gruyère or Cheddar cheese in a large jug (pitcher), then stir in the hot stock. Season well and pour the mixture over the cabbage and pasta, so that it comes about halfway up the dish. If necessary, add a little more stock.

**5** Cover tightly with foil or a lid and bake for 30–35 minutes, until the cabbage is crisp-tender and the stock is bubbling. Remove the lid for the last 5 minutes of the cooking time to brown the top.

# Penne Rigati with Cauliflower

Give cauliflower cheese a twist by adding your favourite pasta shapes.

**Serves 6**

1 medium cauliflower, separated
  into florets
500g/1 ¼ lb/5 cups dried penne
  rigati or other short pasta
500ml/17fl oz/generous
  2 cups milk
1 bay leaf
50g/2oz/ ¼ cup butter
50g/2oz/ ½ cup plain (all-
  purpose) flour
75g/3oz/1 cup freshly grated
  Parmesan or Cheddar cheese
salt and freshly ground
  black pepper

**1** Bring a large pan of lightly salted water to the boil and cook the cauliflower florets for 8–10 minutes, until they are just tender. Remove them from the pan with a slotted spoon. Chop the cauliflower into bitesize pieces and set aside.

**2** Bring the cooking water back to the boil and cook the pasta until it is *al dente*.

**3** Heat the milk with the bay leaf, either in a pan on the hob (stovetop) or in the microwave. Melt the butter in a heavy pan. Add the flour, and cook, stirring constantly, for 1–2 minutes. Remove the bay leaf from the milk. Gradually add the milk to the butter and flour mixture, stirring constantly, until the sauce boils and thickens.

**4** Stir the cheese into the sauce, then fold in the cauliflower. Season with plenty of salt and pepper.

**5** Drain the pasta and return it to the clean pan. Add the cheese and cauliflower sauce and toss to mix. Serve immediately in warmed bowls.

> **Cook's Tip**
> *Save some of the cheese for topping the pasta, if you like, or offer extra at the table.*

# Spaghetti with Ratatouille Sauce

Rich, colourful and robust, this famous provençal vegetable ratatouille makes a superb sauce for spaghetti or shaped pasta.

**Serves 4**
30ml/2 tbsp olive oil
1 onion, sliced
1 garlic clove, chopped
2 courgettes (zucchini), sliced
1 large aubergine (eggplant), cut
   into large chunks
30ml/2 tbsp tomato
   purée (paste)
400g/14oz can
   chopped tomatoes
30ml/2 tbsp chopped fresh
   mixed herbs
350g/12oz dried spaghetti
salt and freshly ground
   black pepper
fresh flat leaf parsley sprigs,
   to garnish
freshly grated Parmesan cheese,
   to serve

**1** Heat the oil in a large, heavy pan. Add the onion and fry over a medium heat, stirring frequently, for 5 minutes, until softened. Add the garlic, courgettes and aubergine, and cook, stirring occasionally, for 2 minutes more.

**2** Stir in the tomato purée, chopped tomatoes and mixed herbs and season with salt and pepper to taste. Bring to the boil, then lower the heat and simmer, stirring occasionally, for 20–30 minutes, until the mixture has thickened and the vegetables are very tender.

**3** Meanwhile, bring a large pan of lightly salted water to the boil and cook the pasta until it is *al dente*.

**4** Drain the pasta well, return it to the clean pan and add the ratatouille. Toss to coat. Serve immediately in warmed bowls, garnished with the fresh flat leaf parsley. Hand around a bowl of freshly grated Parmesan cheese.

> **Variation**
> *For extra colour and flavour, add a sliced orange (bell) pepper with the onion in step 1.*

# Pappardelle Tossed with Grilled Vegetables

A hearty dish to be eaten with crusty bread and washed down with a robust red wine.

**Serves 4**
1 aubergine (eggplant)
2 courgettes (zucchini)
1 red (bell) pepper
8 garlic cloves, unpeeled
about 150ml/¼ pint/⅔ cup
   extra virgin olive oil
450g/1lb dried pappardelle
salt and freshly ground
   black pepper
a few fresh thyme sprigs,
   to garnish

**1** Preheat the grill (broiler). Slice the aubergine and courgettes lengthways. Cut the pepper in half, cut out the stalk and white pith and scrape out the seeds. Slice the pepper lengthways into eight pieces.

**2** Arrange the vegetables and unpeeled garlic cloves in a single layer in a grill pan. Brush liberally with some of the oil and season with salt and pepper. Grill (broil) until the vegetables are slightly charred and the garlic is soft, turning once.

**3** Set the garlic cloves aside to cool slightly. Put the grilled vegetables in a bowl, add the remaining olive oil and toss well to coat. Pop the garlic flesh out of the skins and add it to the vegetable mixture.

**4** Bring a large pan of lightly salted water to the boil and cook the pasta until *al dente*. Drain well, return to the clean pan and add the vegetable mixture. Serve immediately, garnished with the thyme.

> **Cook's Tip**
> *• If you can locate baby aubergines (eggplants) and courgettes (zucchini), so much the better. Use two to three aubergines and about six courgettes.*

# Mushroom & Chilli Carbonara

Dried porcini mushrooms intensify the flavour of this simple dish, while chilli flakes add a spicy undertone.

**Serves 4**
15g/½oz dried
  porcini mushrooms
300ml/ ½ pint/1¼ cups
  hot water
225g/8oz dried spaghetti
25g/1oz/2 tbsp butter
15ml/1 tbsp olive oil
1 garlic clove, crushed
225g/8oz/3 cups button (white)
  or chestnut mushrooms, sliced
5ml/1 tsp dried chilli flakes
2 eggs
300ml/ ½ pint/1¼ cups
  single (light) cream
salt and freshly ground
  black pepper
freshly shaved Parmesan cheese
  and chopped fresh parsley,
  to garnish

**1** Put the dried mushrooms in a bowl. Add the hot water and soak for 15 minutes, then drain and reserve the soaking liquid.

**2** Bring a large pan of lightly salted water to the boil and cook the spaghetti until it is *al dente*. Drain, rinse under cold water and drain again.

**3** Melt the butter and the olive oil in a large, heavy pan and sauté the crushed garlic for 30 seconds. Add the sliced fresh mushrooms, together with the drained porcini, and the dried chilli flakes and stir well. Cook over a medium heat for about 2 minutes, stirring occasionally.

**4** Increase the heat. Pour in the reserved mushroom soaking liquid, bring to the boil and cook over a high heat until the mushroom liquid has reduced slightly.

**5** Beat the eggs and cream in a bowl and season well. Add the cooked spaghetti to the mushroom mixture in the pan and heat through.

**6** Add the egg mixture and toss over the heat for just long enough to cook it lightly and coat the pasta. Serve in warmed bowls, sprinkled with the Parmesan and parsley.

# Pasta & Mushroom Mould

A crisp crumb coating contrasts beautifully with the tender pasta and mushrooms in this bake.

**Serves 4–6**
600ml/1 pint/2½ cups milk
1 bay leaf
1 small onion stuck with 6 cloves
15g/ ½ oz dried
  porcini mushrooms
300ml/ ½ pint/1¼ cups
  hot water
200g/7oz/1¾ cups dried
  pasta shapes
50g/2oz/ ¼ cup butter
45ml/3 tbsp fresh
  white breadcrumbs
10ml/2 tsp dried mixed herbs
40g/1½oz/ ⅓ cup plain (all-
  purpose) flour
60ml/4 tbsp freshly grated
  Parmesan cheese
freshly grated nutmeg
2 eggs, beaten
30ml/2 tbsp olive oil
350g/12oz/4 cups button (white)
  mushrooms, sliced
2 garlic cloves, crushed
30ml/2 tbsp chopped
  fresh parsley
salt and freshly ground
  black pepper

**1** Pour the milk into a pan, and add the bay leaf and clove-studded onion. Bring to just below the boil, then remove the pan from the heat and set aside for 15 minutes.

**2** Meanwhile, put the porcini mushrooms in a second bowl, pour over the hot water and soak for 15 minutes.

**3** Meanwhile, bring a large pan of lightly salted water to the boil and cook the pasta until it is *al dente*.

**4** Melt the butter in a pan over a low heat and use a little to brush the inside of a large oval pie dish. Mix the breadcrumbs and dried mixed herbs together, and use them to coat the inside of the dish.

**5** Remove the onion and bay leaf from the milk and discard. Stir the flour into the remaining melted butter, cook over a low heat, stirring constantly, for 1 minute, then gradually add the milk, stirring constantly until the sauce boils and thickens.

**6** Stir the cheese into the sauce, and season with nutmeg, salt and pepper to taste. Drain the pasta and stir it into the sauce. Cool for 5 minutes, then beat in the eggs.

**7** Drain the porcini, reserving the soaking liquid. Heat the oil in a pan and fry the porcini, button mushrooms and garlic over a medium heat, stirring occasionally, for about 3 minutes. Season with salt and pepper to taste, stir in the reserved soaking liquid and cook over a high heat until it has reduced a little. Stir in the chopped parsley.

**8** Preheat the oven to 190°C/375°F/Gas 5. Spoon a layer of the pasta mixture into the crumb-coated dish. Sprinkle over a thin layer of the mushrooms. Repeat the layers until all the ingredients are used up, finishing with a layer of the pasta mixture. Cover with a sheet of greased foil and transfer to the oven. Bake for 30 minutes. Allow to stand for 5 minutes before turning out to serve.

# Creamy Tagliatelle with Spinach

The most unlikely combinations can prove surprisingly successful, a fact that is amply illustrated in this delicious dish. Italian pasta and spinach, Chinese soy sauce and cheese are mixed here to make this wonderful and mouthwatering dish.

**Serves 4**

225g/8oz fresh leaf
   spinach, trimmed
225g/8oz dried tagliatelle,
   preferably mixed colours
30ml/2 tbsp light soy sauce
75g/3oz garlic and herb cheese
45ml/3 tbsp milk
salt and freshly ground
   black pepper

**1** Remove any tough stalks from the spinach, then wash the leaves well in cold water. Place them in a heavy pan with just the water that clings to the leaves. Cover the pan tightly and cook the spinach until it has just wilted. Drain it very well, using the back of a wooden spoon to press out the excess liquid. Chop the leaves roughly with kitchen scissors.

**2** Bring a large pan of lightly salted water to the boil and cook the pasta until it is *al dente*.

**3** Meanwhile, put the spinach in a frying pan and stir in the soy sauce over a low heat. Add the garlic and herb cheese and stir in the milk. Gradually bring to the boil, stirring constantly until smooth. Season to taste with salt and pepper.

**4** Drain the pasta, return it to the clean pan and pour over the sauce. Toss to mix, then serve in warmed bowls.

---

**Variations**
• *This dish would also work well with watercress, sorrel, rocket (arugula) or radicchio instead of spinach.*
• *If you don't like garlic, use unflavoured Boursin or crumbled feta and stir in 15ml/1 tbsp chopped fresh herbs.*

---

# Fusilli with Peppers & Onions

Grilled peppers have a delicious smoky flavour, and look very colourful in this simple dish.

**Serves 4**

2 large (bell) peppers
400g/14oz/3½ cups dried fusilli
90ml/6 tbsp olive oil
1 large red onion, thinly sliced
2 garlic cloves, crushed
45ml/3 tbsp finely chopped
   fresh parsley
salt and freshly ground
   black pepper
freshly grated Parmesan cheese,
   to serve

**1** Preheat the grill (broiler). Cut the peppers in half, remove the cores and seeds, and place them cut side down in the grill pan. Grill (broil) until the skins have blistered and begun to char.

**2** Put the peppers in a bowl, cover with several layers of kitchen paper and set aside for 10 minutes. Peel off the skins and slice the flesh into thin strips.

**3** Bring a large pan of lightly salted water to the boil and cook the pasta until it is *al dente*.

**4** Heat the oil in a frying pan. Add the onion and fry over a medium heat, stirring frequently, until it is translucent. Stir in the garlic and cook for 2 minutes over a low heat.

**5** Add the peppers and mix gently. Stir in about 45ml/3 tbsp of the pasta cooking water. Stir in the parsley and season the mixture with salt and pepper to taste.

**6** Drain the pasta. Tip it into the pan with the vegetables and toss thoroughly to coat. Serve in warmed bowls, with the Parmesan passed separately.

---

**Cook's Tip**
*Use red and yellow (bell) peppers, or mix red with orange. For a dramatic effect, look out for dark purple peppers.*

# Spaghetti with Black Olive & Mushroom Sauce

Spaghetti gets star treatment, thanks to a rich pungent sauce topped with sweet cherry tomatoes.

**Serves 4**

15ml/1 tbsp olive oil
1 garlic clove, chopped
225g/8oz/3 cups
   mushrooms, chopped

150g/5oz/1¼ cups pitted black
   olives, coarsely chopped
30ml/2 tbsp chopped
   fresh parsley
1 fresh red chilli, seeded
   and chopped
225g/8oz cherry tomatoes
450g/1lb dried spaghetti
slivers of Parmesan cheese,
   to serve

**1** Heat the olive oil in a large, heavy pan. Add the garlic and cook, stirring occasionally, for 1 minute over a low heat. Increase the heat slightly, stir in the mushrooms, cover and cook for a further 5 minutes.

**2** Tip the mushroom mixture into a blender or food processor and add the olives, parsley and red chilli. Process the mixture until smooth.

**3** Heat an ungreased frying pan and add the cherry tomatoes. Shake the pan gently until the tomato skins start to split. Lower the heat to the lowest setting to keep the tomatoes hot while you cook the pasta.

**4** Bring a large pan of lightly salted water to the boil and cook the pasta until it is *al dente*.

**5** Drain the pasta, return it to the pan and add the olive mixture. Toss over the heat until the pasta is coated and the sauce is hot. Serve on warmed plates, topped with the tomatoes and garnished with slivers of Parmesan.

# Spaghetti with Mixed Mushroom & Basil Sauce

Taking its inspiration from Stroganoff, this mushroom and sour cream sauce is very good with spaghetti.

**Serves 4**

50g/2oz/¼ cup butter
1 onion, chopped
350g/12oz/5 cups mixed
   mushrooms, such as brown, flat
   and button (white), sliced

1 garlic clove, chopped
350g/12oz dried spaghetti
300ml/½ pint/1¼ cups
   sour cream
30ml/2 tbsp chopped fresh basil
50g/2oz/⅔ cup freshly grated
   Parmesan cheese, plus extra
   to serve
salt and freshly ground
   black pepper
torn flat leaf parsley, to garnish

**1** Melt the butter in a large, heavy frying pan. Add the onion and fry over a low heat, stirring occasionally, for about 10 minutes.

**2** Add the mushrooms and garlic to the pan and fry, stirring occasionally, for 10 minutes more.

**3** Meanwhile, bring a large pan of lightly salted water to the boil and cook the pasta until *al dente*.

**4** Stir the sour cream into the mushroom mixture, with the basil and Parmesan. Season with plenty of salt and pepper, cover and heat through.

**5** Drain the pasta and tip it into a warmed serving bowl. Add the mushroom and basil sauce and toss thoroughly to mix. Garnish with the flat leaf parsley. Serve immediately with plenty of Parmesan cheese.

> **Variation**
> *Tarragon also complements mushrooms. As it is very pungent, use only 15ml/1 tbsp chopped fresh tarragon.*

# Mushroom Bolognese

A quick – and exceedingly tasty – vegetarian version of the classic Italian meat dish. Use cultivated or wild mushrooms or a mixture.

**Serves 4**

15ml/1 tbsp olive oil
1 onion, chopped
1 garlic clove, crushed
450g/1lb/6 cups mushrooms
15ml/1 tbsp tomato purée (paste)
400g/14oz can
   chopped tomatoes
15ml/1 tbsp chopped
   fresh oregano, plus extra
   to garnish
450g/1lb fresh spaghetti
salt and freshly ground
   black pepper
shavings of Parmesan cheese,
   to serve

**1** Heat the oil in a large, heavy pan. Add the chopped onion and garlic, and cook over a medium heat, stirring occasionally, for 2–3 minutes.

**2** Meanwhile, trim the mushroom stems neatly, then cut each mushroom into quarters. Add the mushrooms to the pan and cook over a high heat for 3–4 minutes, stirring occasionally.

**3** Stir in the tomato purée, chopped tomatoes and oregano. Lower the heat, cover and cook for 5 minutes.

**4** Meanwhile, bring a large pan of lightly salted water to the boil and cook the pasta until *al dente*.

**5** Season the mushroom sauce with salt and pepper to taste. Drain the pasta, tip it into a bowl and add the mushroom mixture. Toss thoroughly to mix. Serve in warmed bowls, topped with shavings of Parmesan and a sprinkling of extra chopped fresh oregano.

> **Cook's Tip**
> *If you prefer to use dried pasta, make this the first thing that you cook. It will take 10–12 minutes, during which time you can make the mushroom mixture. Use 350g/12oz dried pasta.*

# Tagliatelle with Mushrooms

This is a lovely, moist dish with loads of flavour. It is also pleasingly low in fat.

**Serves 4**

1 small onion, finely chopped
2 garlic cloves, crushed
150ml/¼ pint/⅔ cup
   Vegetable Stock
225g/8oz/3 cups mixed fresh
   mushrooms, such as field,
   chestnut, oyster or
   chanterelles, quartered
60ml/4 tbsp white or red wine
10ml/2 tsp tomato purée (paste)
15ml/1 tbsp soy sauce
225g/8oz fresh sun-dried tomato
   and herb tagliatelle
5ml/1 tsp chopped fresh thyme
30ml/2 tbsp chopped
   fresh parsley
salt and freshly ground
   black pepper
shavings of Parmesan cheese, to
   serve (optional)

**1** Put the onion and garlic into a pan with the stock. Cover and cook over a medium heat for 5 minutes, or until tender.

**2** Stir in the mushrooms, wine, tomato purée and soy sauce. Cover and cook for 5 minutes.

**3** Remove the lid from the pan and increase the heat. Bring to the boil and boil until the liquid has reduced by half. Season with salt and pepper to taste.

**4** Meanwhile, bring a large pan of lightly salted water to the boil and cook the pasta until it is *al dente*.

**5** Drain the pasta, return it to the clean pan and toss lightly with the mushroom mixture and chopped herbs. Serve immediately, with shavings of Parmesan cheese, if you like.

> **Cook's Tip**
> *Mushrooms are best eaten as fresh as possible, as they do not store well and quickly lose their texture. Cultivated varieties will keep in the refrigerator for up to 3 days; wild mushrooms for 1–2 days. Store them in a paper bag, not plastic.*

# Somen Noodles with Courgettes

This is a colourful dish packed with lots of flavour – absolutely perfect for a midweek family supper. Pumpkin or patty pan squash can be used instead of the courgettes.

### Serves 4
2 yellow courgettes (zucchini)
2 green courgettes (zucchini)
60ml/4 tbsp pine nuts
60ml/4 tbsp extra virgin olive oil
2 shallots, finely chopped
2 garlic cloves, finely chopped
30ml/2 tbsp bottled capers, rinsed and drained
4 drained sun-dried tomatoes in oil, cut into strips
300g/11oz dried somen noodles
60ml/4 tbsp chopped mixed fresh herbs
grated rind of 1 lemon
50g/2oz/ $^2/_3$ cup freshly grated Parmesan cheese
salt and freshly ground black pepper

**1** Slice the courgettes diagonally into rounds, making them roughly the same thickness as the noodles, then cut the slices into thin batons.

**2** Toast the pine nuts in an ungreased frying pan over a medium heat until golden in colour.

**3** Heat half the oil in a large frying pan. Add the shallots and garlic, and fry until fragrant. Push the shallot mixture to the side of the pan, add the remaining oil and, when hot, stir-fry the courgettes until soft.

**4** Stir thoroughly to incorporate the shallot mixture and add the capers, sun-dried tomatoes and pine nuts. Remove the pan from the heat.

**5** Bring a large pan of lightly salted water to the boil and cook the noodles until just tender. Drain well.

**6** Toss the noodles into the courgette mixture and add the herbs, lemon rind and Parmesan. Season with salt and pepper to taste, and toss over the heat for 1–2 minutes. Transfer to a warmed serving bowl and serve immediately.

# Somen Noodles with Baked Cherry Tomatoes

This summery dish is bursting with flavour. Baking the cherry tomatoes slowly strengthens their taste. If you can find yellow cherry tomatoes, use a mixture of red and yellow for an extra-special touch.

### Serves 4–6
1kg/2¼lb cherry tomatoes
3 garlic cloves, finely sliced
1 bunch of fresh basil
120ml/4fl oz/ ½ cup extra virgin olive oil
450g/1lb dried somen noodles
salt and freshly ground black pepper
shavings of Parmesan cheese and tiny basil sprigs, to garnish

**1** Preheat the oven to 180°C/350°F/Gas 4. Cut the tomatoes in half and arrange them, cut side up, in a single layer in an ovenproof dish. Season with salt and pepper to taste and sprinkle with sliced garlic.

**2** Strip the basil leaves from the stems, then arrange half of them over the tomatoes. Drizzle half the olive oil over the top. Bake the tomatoes for 1–1½ hours. Set aside and keep warm until ready to serve.

**3** Just before serving, bring a large pan of lightly salted water to the boil and cook the somen noodles until just tender. Drain well, tip into a bowl and toss lightly with the baked tomatoes and their juices.

**4** Add the remaining basil, with more olive oil and seasoning. Serve immediately, garnished with Parmesan shavings and a few basil sprigs.

### Cook's Tip
*Take care when tossing the mixture that you don't break up the baked tomatoes too much.*

# Crispy Noodles with Mixed Vegetables

In this dish, rice vermicelli noodles are deep-fried until crisp, then tossed into a colourful selection of stir-fried vegetables.

### Serves 3–4
2 large carrots
2 courgettes (zucchini)
4 spring onions (scallions)
115g/4oz yard-long beans or green beans
115g/4oz dried vermicelli rice noodles or cellophane noodles
groundnut (peanut) oil, for deep-frying

2.5cm/1in piece of fresh root ginger, shredded
1 fresh red chilli, sliced
115g/4oz/1½ cups fresh shiitake or button (white) mushrooms, thickly sliced
a few Chinese cabbage leaves, coarsely shredded
75g/3oz/⅓ cup beansprouts
30ml/2 tbsp light soy sauce
30ml/2 tbsp Chinese rice wine or dry sherry
5ml/1 tsp granulated sugar
30ml/2 tbsp roughly torn coriander (cilantro) leaves

**1** Cut the carrots and courgettes into fine sticks. Shred the spring onions into similar-size pieces. Trim the beans. If using yard-long beans, cut them into short lengths. Break the noodles into lengths of about 7.5cm/3in.

**2** Half-fill a wok with oil and heat it to 180°C/350°F. Deep-fry the noodles, a handful at a time, for 1–2 minutes, until puffed and crispy. Lift out with a slotted spoon and drain on kitchen paper. Carefully pour off all but 30ml/2 tbsp of the oil.

**3** Reheat the oil in the wok. When hot, add the beans and stir-fry for 2–3 minutes. Add the ginger, chilli, mushrooms, carrots and courgettes and stir-fry for 1–2 minutes.

**4** Add the Chinese cabbage, beansprouts and spring onions. Stir-fry for 1 minute, then add the soy sauce, rice wine or sherry and sugar. Cook, stirring, for about 30 seconds. Add the noodles and coriander and toss, taking care not to crush the noodles. Pile on a warm serving plate and serve immediately.

# Noodle Cakes with Vegetables

Slightly crisp noodle cakes topped with vegetables make a superb dish.

### Serves 4
175g/6oz dried egg vermicelli
15ml/1 tbsp vegetable oil
2 garlic cloves, finely chopped
115g/4oz/⅔ cup baby corn cobs, halved lengthways
115g/4oz/1½ cups fresh shiitake mushrooms, halved
3 celery sticks, sliced
1 carrot, diagonally sliced
115g/4oz/1 cup mangetouts (snow peas)

75g/3oz/¾ cup drained canned sliced bamboo shoots
15ml/1 tbsp cornflour (cornstarch), mixed to a paste with 15ml/1 tbsp water
15ml/1 tbsp dark soy sauce
5ml/1 tsp caster (superfine) sugar
300ml/½ pint/1¼ cups Vegetable Stock
salt and freshly ground white pepper
spring onion (scallion) curls, to garnish

**1** Bring a pan of lightly salted water to the boil and cook the egg vermicelli briefly until just tender. Drain, refresh under cold water, drain again, then dry thoroughly on kitchen paper.

**2** Heat 2.5ml/½ tsp of the oil in a non-stick frying pan. When it is very hot, spread half the noodles over the base. Fry for 2–3 minutes until the noodles are lightly toasted and have stuck together to form a cake. Carefully turn this over, fry the other side, then slide the noodle cake on to a heated serving plate. Make a second cake from the remaining noodles. Keep hot.

**3** Heat the remaining oil in the clean pan, then fry the garlic for a few seconds. Add the corn cobs and mushrooms, and stir-fry for 3 minutes over a medium heat. Add the celery, carrot, mangetouts and bamboo shoots. Stir-fry for 2 minutes, or until the vegetables are crisp-tender.

**4** Stir in the cornflour paste, soy sauce, sugar and stock. Cook, stirring, until the sauce thickens. Season with salt and pepper to taste. Divide the vegetable mixture among the noodle cakes, garnish with the spring onion curls and serve immediately.

# Chinese Mushrooms with Cellophane Noodles

Red fermented beancurd adds extra flavour to this hearty vegetarian dish.

**Serves 4**

115g/4oz Chinese
   dried mushrooms
25g/1oz dried wood ears
115g/4oz dried beancurd (tofu)
30ml/2 tbsp vegetable oil
2 garlic cloves, finely chopped
2 slices of fresh root ginger,
   finely chopped
10 Sichuan
   peppercorns, crushed
15ml/1 tbsp red fermented
   beancurd (tofu)
$^1/_2$ star anise
pinch of granulated sugar
15–30ml/1–2 tbsp soy sauce
50g/2oz cellophane noodles,
   soaked in hot water until soft
salt

**1** Soak the Chinese mushrooms and wood ears separately in bowls of hot water for 30 minutes. Break the dried beancurd into small pieces and soak it in water, following the instructions on the packet.

**2** Strain the mushrooms, reserving the liquid. Squeeze as much liquid from the mushrooms as possible, then discard the mushroom stems. Cut the cups in half if they are large.

**3** The wood ears should swell to five times their original size. Drain them, rinse thoroughly and drain again. Cut off any gritty parts, then cut each wood ear into two or three pieces.

**4** Heat the oil in a heavy pan. Add the garlic, ginger and Sichuan peppercorns. Fry for a few seconds, then add the mushrooms and red fermented beancurd. Mix lightly and fry, stirring occasionally, for 5 minutes.

**5** Add the reserved mushroom liquid to the pan, with sufficient water to cover the mushrooms completely. Add the star anise, sugar and soy sauce, then cover and simmer for 30 minutes.

**6** Add the chopped wood ears and reconstituted beancurd pieces to the pan. Cover and cook for about 10 minutes.

**7** Drain the cellophane noodles, add them to the mixture and cook for 10 minutes more, until tender, adding more liquid if necessary. Add salt to taste and serve.

> **Cook's Tip**
> Brick red in colour, red fermented beancurd (tofu) has a very strong, cheese flavour, and is fermented with salt, red rice and rice wine. Look for it in Chinese food stores.

> **Variation**
> If you can't find Sichuan peppercorns, then use ordinary black ones instead.

# Fried Noodles with Beancurd

Fried potatoes and beancurd are both excellent vehicles for the spicy flavours in this unusual stir-fry.

**Serves 4**

2 eggs
60ml/4 tbsp vegetable oil
5ml/1 tsp chilli powder
5ml/1 tsp ground turmeric
1 large onion, finely sliced
2 fresh red chillies, seeded and
   finely sliced
15ml/1 tbsp soy sauce
2 large cooked potatoes, cut into
   small cubes
6 pieces of fried beancurd
   (tofu), sliced
225g/8oz/4 cups beansprouts
115g/4oz green beans, blanched
350g/12oz fresh thick
   egg noodles
salt and freshly ground
   black pepper
sliced spring onions (scallions),
   to garnish

**1** Beat the eggs lightly in a bowl. Heat an omelette pan and grease it lightly with a little of the oil. Use half the egg mixture to make a thin omelette. Slide it on to a plate, blot it with kitchen paper, roll it up and cut it into narrow strips. Make a second omelette in the same way and slice. Set the omelette strips aside for the garnish.

**2** In a cup, mix together the chilli powder and turmeric. Form a paste by stirring in a little water.

**3** Preheat a wok and swirl in the remaining oil. Add the onion and stir-fry over a medium heat until soft. Reduce the heat and add the chilli paste, sliced chillies and soy sauce. Stir-fry for 2–3 minutes.

**4** Add the potatoes and stir-fry for about 2 minutes, mixing them well with the chillies. Add the beancurd, then the beansprouts, green beans and noodles.

**5** Gently stir-fry over a low heat until the noodles are evenly coated and heated through. Take care not to break up the potatoes or the beancurd. Season with salt and pepper to taste. Serve hot, garnished with the reserved omelette strips and spring onion slices.

# Rice Noodles with Vegetable Chilli Sauce

Vegetable chilli is often served with baked potatoes or rice. Teaming it with noodles is inspirational.

**Serves 4**

15ml/1 tbsp sunflower oil
1 onion, chopped
2 garlic cloves, crushed
1 fresh red chilli, seeded and finely chopped
1 red (bell) pepper, seeded and diced
2 carrots, finely chopped
175g/6oz/1 cup baby corn cobs, halved
225g/8oz can sliced bamboo shoots, rinsed and drained
400g/14oz can red kidney beans, rinsed and drained
300ml/ ½ pint/1 ¼ cups passata (bottled strained tomatoes)
15ml/1 tbsp soy sauce
5ml/1 tsp ground coriander
250g/9oz dried rice noodles
30ml/2 tbsp chopped fresh parsley, plus parsley sprigs, to garnish
salt and freshly ground black pepper

**1** Heat the oil in a large pan. and cook the onion, garlic, chilli and red pepper, stirring occasionally, for 5 minutes.

**2** Stir in the carrots, corn cobs, bamboo shoots, kidney beans, passata, soy sauce and ground coriander.

**3** Bring to the boil, then cover, lower the heat and simmer gently for 30 minutes, until the vegetables are tender, stirring occasionally. Season with salt and pepper to taste.

**4** Meanwhile, put the rice noodles in a bowl and pour over sufficient boiling water to cover them. Stir with a fork and leave to stand for 3–4 minutes, or according to the packet instructions. Drain, then rinse with boiling water and drain thoroughly again.

**5** Stir the parsley into the sauce. Spoon the noodles on to warmed serving plates and top with the sauce. Garnish with the parsley and serve immediately.

# Vegetable & Egg Noodle Ribbons

Serve this elegant, colourful dish with a tossed green salad as a light lunch for four or as an appetizer for six to eight people.

**Serves 4–8**

1 large carrot
2 courgettes (zucchini)
50g/2oz/ ¼ cup butter
15ml/1 tbsp olive oil
6 fresh shiitake mushrooms, thinly sliced
50g/2oz/ ½ cup frozen peas, thawed
350g/12oz broad dried egg noodles
10ml/2 tsp chopped mixed herbs, such as marjoram, chives and basil
salt and freshly ground black pepper
25g/1oz Parmesan cheese, to serve (optional)

**1** Using a vegetable peeler, carefully slice thin strips from the carrot and from the courgettes.

**2** Heat the butter with the olive oil in a large frying pan. Add the carrot and shiitake mushrooms and fry, stirring frequently, for 2 minutes. Add the courgettes and peas and stir-fry until the courgettes are cooked, but still crisp. Season with salt and pepper to taste.

**3** Meanwhile, bring a large pan of lightly salted water to the boil and cook the noodles briefly until just tender. Drain them well and tip them into a warmed serving bowl. Add the vegetables and toss to mix.

**4** Sprinkle over the fresh herbs and season to taste. If using the Parmesan cheese, grate or shave it over the top. Toss lightly and serve immediately.

## Cook's Tip
*The noodles you want here are the Chinese broad flat ribbons, which are available from Asian markets. However, pappardelle could be used instead.*

# SPECIAL OCCASIONS

As it is so popular with young and old alike, pasta is always an excellent choice for celebration suppers and for entertaining guests. It's a good way of adding a touch of luxury to a meal, as you can splash out on one or two special ingredients, such as artichokes, asparagus or a particularly fine cheese, while the rest of the dish is very economical. Home-made pasta is always a treat and will not only impress your guests, but also make them feel especially welcome. This chapter features some simply stunning recipes for filled pasta that will turn any occasion into a feast. While they often take quite a long time to prepare, all of the fiddly work can be done before your guests arrive. For really easy entertaining, serve one of the superb baked dishes, such as Leek & Chèvre Lasagne, which can be ready for popping into the oven as the doorbell rings. Alternatively, you could choose one of the many quick and easy, but equally delicious and elegant recipes also included here. Ideal for informal entertaining, dishes such as Garganelli with Asparagus, Wine & Cream can be prepared in just the time it takes the pasta to cook.

Many of the recipes in this chapter – whether appetizers or main-course dishes – have been inspired by the menus of Rome's sophisticated restaurants, whose clientele include some of the most discriminating diners in the world.

# Penne with Artichokes

This sauce is rich and makes this dish a superb dinner-party appetizer.

**Serves 6**
juice of 1 lemon
2 globe artichokes
30ml/2 tbsp olive oil
1 small fennel bulb, thinly sliced, with feathery tops reserved
1 onion, finely chopped
4 garlic cloves, finely chopped
1 handful fresh flat leaf parsley, roughly chopped
400g/14oz can chopped Italian plum tomatoes
150ml/ ¼ pint/ ⅔ cup dry white wine
350g/12oz/3 cups dried penne
10ml/2 tsp capers, chopped
salt and freshly ground black pepper
freshly grated Parmesan cheese, to serve

**1** Stir half the lemon juice into a bowl of cold water. Cut off the artichoke stalks, then discard the outer leaves. Cut off the tops of the inner leaves so that the base remains. Cut the base in half lengthways, then prise the choke out of the centre with the tip of a knife and discard. Cut the artichokes lengthways into 5mm/ ¼in slices, adding them to the bowl of acidulated water.

**2** Bring a large pan of water to the boil. Add a pinch of salt, then drain the artichokes and add them immediately to the water. Boil for 5 minutes, drain and set aside.

**3** Heat the oil in a large pan and cook the fennel, onion, garlic and parsley over a low heat for 10 minutes.

**4** Add the tomatoes and wine with salt and pepper. Bring to the boil, stirring, then simmer for 15 minutes. Stir in the artichokes, replace the lid and simmer for 10 minutes more.

**5** Meanwhile, bring a pan of lightly salted water to the boil and cook the pasta until it is *al dente*. Stir the capers into the tomato sauce, then add the remaining lemon juice.

**6** Tip the pasta into a warmed large bowl, pour the sauce over and toss. Serve immediately, garnished with the reserved fennel fronds. Hand around a bowl of grated Parmesan separately.

# Pasta with Coriander & Grilled Aubergines

Pasta with a piquant sauce of coriander and lime is superb with succulent grilled aubergines.

**Serves 2**
15g/½ oz/ ½ cup coriander (cilantro) leaves
30ml/2 tbsp pine nuts
30ml/2 tbsp freshly grated Parmesan cheese
3 garlic cloves
juice of ½ lime
105ml/7 tbsp olive oil
225g/8oz/2 cups dried cellentani or other pasta shapes
1 large aubergine (eggplant)
salt and freshly ground black pepper

**1** Process the coriander leaves, pine nuts, Parmesan, garlic, lime juice and 60ml/4 tbsp of the olive oil in a food processor or blender for 30 seconds, until almost smooth.

**2** Bring a pan of lightly salted water to the boil and cook the pasta until it is *al dente*.

**3** Meanwhile, cut the aubergine in half lengthways, then cut each half into 5mm/ ¼in slices. Layer the aubergine strips in a colander with salt and leave to stand for 30 minutes over a plate to catch any juices. Rinse off the excess salt under cold water and drain.

**4** Spread the slices out on a baking sheet, brush with half the remaining oil and season well with salt and black pepper.

**5** Grill (broil) the aubergine slices for about 4 minutes. Turn them over and brush them with the remaining oil. Season as before. Grill for 4 minutes more.

**6** Drain the pasta, tip it into a warmed bowl and toss with the coriander sauce. Serve with the grilled aubergine slices.

# Tagliolini with Asparagus

Tagliolini are very thin home-made egg noodles. They go well with this subtle cream sauce flavoured with asparagus.

**Serves 4**

450g/1lb fresh
  asparagus, trimmed
50g/2oz/ $^1/_4$ cup butter
3 spring onions (scallions),
  finely chopped
3–4 fresh mint leaves,
  finely chopped
150ml/ $^1/_4$ pint/ $^2/_3$ cup
  double (heavy) cream
350g/12oz fresh tagliolini or
  other egg noodles
50g/2oz/ $^2/_3$ cup freshly grated
  Parmesan cheese
salt and freshly ground
  black pepper
fresh basil, to garnish

**1** Bring a large pan of lightly salted water to the boil. Add the asparagus spears and boil for 4–6 minutes, until just tender. Using a slotted spoon, lift out the asparagus spears. Cut the tips off, and then cut the stalks into 4cm/1 $^1/_2$in pieces. Set the asparagus aside and reserve the pan of cooking water.

**2** Melt the butter in a large, heavy frying pan. Add the spring onions and mint and cook over a low heat, stirring occasionally, for 3–4 minutes.

**3** Stir in the cream and asparagus, season with salt and pepper to taste and heat gently, but do not boil.

**4** Meanwhile, bring the asparagus cooking water back to the boil and cook the pasta until it is *al dente*.

**5** Drain the pasta well, then add it to the sauce in the frying pan. Raise the heat slightly and mix well. Stir in the Parmesan and serve immediately, garnished with basil leaves.

> **Cook's Tip**
> *If you like, stir only half the Parmesan into the sauce and offer the rest at the table.*

# Garganelli with Asparagus, Wine & Cream

A lovely recipe for late spring when bunches of fresh young asparagus are on sale in stores and markets everywhere.

**Serves 4**

350g/12oz fresh young
  asparagus, trimmed
350g/12oz/3 cups
  dried garganelli
25g/1oz/2 tbsp butter
200ml/7fl oz/scant 1 cup
  double (heavy) cream
30ml/2 tbsp dry white wine
115g/4oz/1 $^1/_3$ cups freshly grated
  Parmesan cheese
30ml/2 tbsp chopped fresh mixed
  herbs, such as basil, flat leaf
  parsley, chervil, marjoram
  and oregano
salt and freshly ground
  black pepper

**1** Cut the asparagus spears diagonally into pieces that are roughly the same length and shape as the garganelli. Keep the tips separate.

**2** Bring a large pan of lightly salted water to the boil. Add all but the tips of the asparagus and cook for 2 minutes, then add the tips and cook for 1 minute more. Working quickly, transfer the asparagus to a colander, using a slotted spoon, and rinse under cold water. Set aside to drain.

**3** Bring the asparagus cooking water back to the boil and cook the pasta until it is *al dente*.

**4** Meanwhile, put the butter and cream in a medium pan, season with salt and pepper to taste and bring to the boil over a low heat. Simmer for a few minutes until the cream has reduced and thickened slightly, then add the asparagus, wine and about half the grated Parmesan. Taste for seasoning and keep on a low heat.

**5** Drain the pasta and tip it into a warmed bowl. Pour the sauce over, sprinkle with the fresh herbs and toss well. Serve immediately, topped with the remaining grated Parmesan.

# Linguine with Rocket

You will often find this traditional Calabrian dish served as an appetizer in fashionable restaurants. It is very quick and easy to make at home and is worth trying for yourself.

**Serves 4**
350g/12oz fresh or dried linguine
120ml/4fl oz/ ½ cup extra virgin
    olive oil
1 large bunch rocket (arugula),
    about 150g/5oz, stalks
    removed, leaves shredded
75g/3oz/1 cup freshly grated
    Parmesan cheese
salt and freshly ground
    black pepper

**1** Bring a large pan of lightly salted water to the boil and cook the pasta until it is *al dente*. Drain.

**2** Heat about half the olive oil in the pasta pan, then add the pasta, followed by the rocket. Fry over a medium to high heat, stirring and tossing constantly, for 1–2 minutes, or until the rocket is just wilted, then remove the pan from the heat.

**3** Tip the pasta and rocket into a warmed large bowl. Add the freshly grated Parmesan and the remaining olive oil. Add a little salt and black pepper to taste.

**4** Toss the mixture quickly to mix and coat the ingredients with the olive oil. Serve immediately.

## Cook's Tips
• Buy rocket (arugula) by the bunch from the greengrocer or, better still, grow it yourself. Use the leaves when they are young and bright green. In hot weather, rocket leaves quickly turn yellow, and older leaves have a distinctly peppery flavour.
• Although cultivated rocket is much less pungent than the wild variety, you may still find its flavour too powerful. If so, blanch the leaves very briefly in boiling water and drain before cooking them in the oil.

# Orecchiette with Tomatoes & Rocket

Serve this hearty dish as a main course with country bread. Some delicatessens and supermarkets sell a farmhouse-style Italian loaf called *pugliese*, which would be perfect.

**Serves 4–6**
45ml/3 tbsp olive oil
1 small onion, finely chopped
300g/11oz canned chopped
    Italian plum tomatoes
2.5ml/ ½ tsp dried oregano
pinch of chilli powder
about 30ml/2 tbsp red wine
2 medium potatoes, diced
300g/11oz/2¾ cups
    dried orecchiette
2 garlic cloves, finely chopped
150g/5oz rocket (arugula), stalks
    removed, leaves shredded
90g/3½ oz/scant ½ cup
    ricotta cheese
salt and freshly ground
    black pepper
freshly grated Pecorino cheese,
    to serve

**1** Heat 15ml/1 tbsp of the olive oil in a pan. Add half the onion and cook, stirring occasionally, for about 5 minutes, until it is softened. Stir in the chopped tomatoes and dried oregano and season with chilli powder to taste. Pour the red wine over and season with salt and pepper to taste. Cover the pan and simmer for about 15 minutes, stirring occasionally.

**2** Bring a large pan of lightly salted water to the boil. Add the potatoes and pasta. Stir well and let the water return to the boil. Lower the heat and simmer for about 15 minutes, or until both the potatoes and the pasta are just tender.

**3** When the pasta and diced potatoes are almost ready, heat the remaining olive oil in a large, heavy pan, add the remaining onion and the garlic, and fry over a medium heat, stirring occasionally, for 2–3 minutes.

**4** Add the rocket, toss over the heat for about 2 minutes, until wilted, then add the tomato sauce and the ricotta. Mix well.

**5** Drain the pasta and potatoes, add both to the pan of sauce and toss to mix. Taste for seasoning and serve immediately in warmed bowls, with grated Pecorino handed separately.

# Rigatoni with Garlic Crumbs

A hot and spicy dish – halve the quantity of chilli if you like a milder flavour.

**Serves 4–6**
45ml/3 tbsp olive oil
2 shallots, chopped
10ml/2 tsp crushed dried chillies
400g/14oz can chopped
  tomatoes with garlic and herbs
6 slices of white bread
115g/4oz/ ½ cup butter
2 garlic cloves, chopped
115g/4oz/1 ½ cups
  sliced mushrooms
450g/1lb/4 cups dried rigatoni
salt and freshly ground
  black pepper
fresh herb sprigs, to garnish

**1** Heat the oil in a pan. Add the shallots and fry over a low heat, stirring occasionally, for 6–8 minutes, until golden. Add the dried chillies and chopped tomatoes, half-cover and simmer for 20 minutes.

**2** Meanwhile, cut the crusts off the bread and discard them. Reduce the bread to crumbs in a food processor. Heat the butter in a frying pan, add the garlic and breadcrumbs and stir-fry until pale golden and crisp.

**3** Stir the mushrooms into the shallot and tomato mixture, season to taste and leave over a low heat while you cook the pasta.

**4** Bring a large pan of lightly salted water to the boil and cook the pasta until it is *al dente*.

**5** Drain the pasta, return it to the clean pan and add the sauce. Toss thoroughly. Divide among four warmed bowls, sprinkle with the garlic crumbs, garnish with the herb sprigs and serve immediately.

**Variations**
*Use sliced drained sun-dried tomatoes in oil instead of the mushrooms, if you like, and a whole fresh red chilli, seeded and chopped, instead of the dried chilli.*

**Cook's Tip**
*It is better to use day-old bread instead of fresh when making crumbs in a food processor, otherwise the bread may form into clumps.*

# Spaghettini with Roasted Garlic

Roasted garlic tastes sweet and is far milder than you would expect, so a whole bulb is not so excessive as it might seem.

**Serves 4**
*whole bulb of garlic*
*120ml/4fl oz/ ½ cup extra virgin*
  *olive oil, plus extra for brushing*
*400g/14oz fresh or*
  *dried spaghettini*
*salt and freshly ground*
  *black pepper*
*coarsely shaved Parmesan cheese,*
  *to serve*

**1** Preheat the oven to 180°C/350°F/Gas 4. Place the garlic in an oiled roasting pan and roast it for 30 minutes. Set it aside to cool slightly.

**2** Bring a pan of lightly salted water to the boil and cook the pasta until it is *al dente*.

**3** Slice off the top third of the bulb of garlic with a sharp knife. Hold the garlic over a bowl and dig out the flesh from each clove with the point of the knife so that it falls into the bowl. Pour in the oil and add plenty of black pepper. Mix well.

**4** Drain the pasta and return it to the clean pan. Pour in the oil and garlic mixture and toss the pasta until all the strands are thoroughly coated. Serve immediately, with shavings of Parmesan handed separately.

**Cook's Tip**
*Although you can now buy roasted garlic in most supermarkets, it is best to roast it yourself for this simple recipe, so that it melts into the olive oil and coats the strands of pasta beautifully. If you can, use the new season's fresh garlic, which is wonderfully plump, tender and sweet. It is usually available from the middle of spring. The purple-skinned variety is considered to have the best flavour.*

# Tagliatelle with Chanterelles

Simplicity is the key to the success of this attractive and sophisticated dish.

**Serves 4**
about 50g/2oz/ ¼ cup butter
225–350g/8–12oz/3–4 cups
   chanterelle mushrooms
15ml/1 tbsp plain (all-
   purpose) flour
150ml/ ¼ pint/ ²⁄₃ cup milk
90ml/6 tbsp crème fraîche
15ml/1 tbsp chopped
   fresh parsley
275g/10oz fresh tagliatelle
salt and freshly ground
   black pepper

**1** Melt 40g/1½oz/3 tbsp of the butter in a large, heavy frying pan. Add the mushrooms and fry for about 2–3 minutes over a gentle heat until the juices begin to run, then increase the heat and cook until the liquid has almost evaporated. Using a slotted spoon, transfer the mushrooms to a bowl.

**2** Stir the flour into the liquid remaining in the pan, adding a little more butter if necessary. Cook, stirring constantly, for about 1 minute and then gradually add the milk, stirring until the sauce boils and thickens. Stir in the crème fraîche and parsley and return the mushrooms to the pan. Season with salt and pepper to taste and stir well. Leave over the lowest possible heat while you cook the pasta.

**3** Bring a large pan of lightly salted water to the boil and cook the pasta until it is *al dente*.

**4** Drain well, return to the clean pan and pour over the mushroom sauce. Toss lightly and serve on warmed plates.

> **Cook's Tip**
> *It is important to clean chanterelles thoroughly. Brush gently with a soft brush, then hold each one by the stalk and let cold water run under the gills to dislodge hidden grit and dirt. Shake gently to dry.*

# Tortellini with Mushroom & Cheese Sauce

A rich sauce of mushrooms and three cheeses coats mouthwatering filled pasta.

**Serves 4**
450g/1lb ricotta-and-spinach-
   filled tortellini
50g/2oz/ ¼ cup butter
2 garlic cloves, chopped
225g/8oz/3 cups field
   (portabello) or button (white)
   mushrooms, sliced
15ml/1 tbsp plain (all-
   purpose) flour
175ml/6fl oz/ ¾ cup milk
50g/2oz/²⁄₃ cup freshly grated
   Parmesan cheese
50g/2oz/ ½ cup grated
   Fontina cheese
115g/4oz/ ²⁄₃ cup ricotta cheese
60ml/4 tbsp single (light) cream
30ml/2 tbsp chopped fresh chives
salt and freshly ground
   black pepper

**1** Bring a large pan of lightly salted water to the boil and cook the tortellini until they are *al dente*.

**2** Melt the butter in a large, heavy frying pan, and fry the garlic and mushrooms for about 5 minutes until browned. Using a slotted spoon, transfer the mushrooms to a bowl.

**3** Add the flour to the butter remaining in the frying pan and cook, stirring constantly, for 1 minute. Gradually add the milk, stirring constantly, until the sauce boils and thickens.

**4** Stir in the Parmesan, Fontina and ricotta cheeses and heat gently until they have melted into the sauce. Return the mushrooms to the sauce and stir in the cream and chives. Season with salt and pepper to taste.

**5** Drain the pasta and tip it into a large serving bowl. Pour over the sauce and toss gently to coat. Serve immediately.

> **Cook's Tip**
> *You can use either plain or spinach-flavoured tortellini.*

# Paglia e Fieno with Radicchio

This is a light, modern pasta dish of the kind served in fashionable restaurants.

**Serves 4**
45ml/3 tbsp pine nuts
350g/12oz dried paglia e fieno
45ml/3 tbsp extra virgin olive oil
30ml/2 tbsp sun-dried
   tomato purée (paste)
2 sun-dried tomatoes in olive oil,
   drained and cut into very
   thin slivers
40g/1½oz radicchio leaves,
   finely shredded
4–6 spring onions (scallions),
   thinly sliced into rings
salt and freshly ground
   black pepper

**1** Put the pine nuts in a non-stick frying pan and toss them over a low to medium heat for 1–2 minutes, or until they are lightly toasted and golden. Remove and set aside.

**2** Bring two pans of lightly salted water to the boil. Add the spinach flavoured pasta to one pan and the plain egg pasta to the other. Cook until both batches are *al dente*.

**3** While the pasta is cooking, heat 15ml/1 tbsp of the olive oil in a pan. Add the sun-dried tomato purée and the sun-dried tomatoes, then stir in 90ml/6 tbsp of the water used for cooking the pasta. Simmer over a low heat until the sauce has reduced slightly, stirring constantly.

**4** Stir in the shredded radicchio, then taste and season if necessary. Keep on a low heat. Drain the paglia e fieno, keeping the colours separate, and return the separate colours to the pans in which they were cooked. Add about 15ml/1 tbsp oil to each pan and toss over a medium to high heat until the pasta is glistening with the oil.

**5** Arrange a portion of green and white pasta in each of four warmed bowls, then spoon the sun-dried tomato and radicchio mixture in the centre. Sprinkle the spring onions and toasted pine nuts decoratively over the top and serve immediately. Before eating, each diner should toss the sauce ingredients with the pasta to mix well.

# Cappelletti with Tomatoes, White Wine & Cream

In this very quick and easy recipe, the sauce coats little filled pasta hats to make a really substantial, creamy supper dish for vegetarians.

**Serves 4–6**
400ml/14fl oz/1⅔ cups passata
   (bottled strained tomatoes)
90ml/6 tbsp dry white wine
150ml/¼ pint/⅔ cup
   double (heavy) cream
225g/8oz/2½ cups
   fresh cappelletti
1 small handful of fresh
   basil leaves
60ml/4 tbsp freshly grated
   Parmesan cheese
salt and freshly ground
   black pepper

**1** Pour the passata into a pan and stir in the wine. Bring to the boil over a medium heat, then stir in the cream until well mixed and bubbling. Lower the heat and simmer for 20 minutes.

**2** Bring a large pan of lightly salted water to the boil and cook the pasta until *al dente*. Meanwhile, finely shred most of the basil leaves and set aside with the whole leaves.

**3** Drain the pasta, return it to the pan and toss it with the grated Parmesan. Pour the sauce over and toss well. Serve sprinkled with the shredded basil and whole basil leaves.

**Cook's Tips**
• *Cappelletti with a variety of fillings are available from supermarkets and Italian delicatessens.*
• *Other stuffed pasta shapes, such as tortellini, ravioli, or the more unusual sacchettini (little purses) or caramellone (toffees), can be used with this sauce.*
• *The tomato sauce can be made up to a day ahead, then chilled until ready to use. Reheat it gently in a heavy pan while the pasta is cooking.*

# Pasta with Caponata

The Sicilians have an excellent sweet and sour vegetable dish called *caponata*, which goes wonderfully well with pasta.

**Serves 4**

60ml/4 tbsp extra virgin olive oil
8 shallots, peeled
2 garlic cloves, crushed
1 large red (bell) pepper, seeded and sliced
1 medium aubergine (eggplant), cut into sticks
2 medium courgettes (zucchini), cut into sticks
450ml/ $^3/_4$ pint/1 $^3/_4$ cups tomato juice
150ml/ $^1/_4$ pint/ $^2/_3$ cup water
30ml/2 tbsp balsamic vinegar
juice of 1 lemon
15ml/1 tbsp granulated sugar
30ml/2 tbsp sliced pitted black olives
30ml/2 tbsp drained capers
400g/14oz fresh or dried tagliatelle
salt and freshly ground black pepper

**1** Heat the oil in a large pan. Add the shallots, garlic and red pepper, and fry over a low heat, stirring occasionally, for 5 minutes. Stir in the aubergine and courgettes and fry, stirring occasionally, for a further 5 minutes.

**2** Stir in the tomato juice and water. Bring to the boil, stirring occasionally, then add the vinegar, lemon juice, sugar, olives and capers. Season with salt and pepper to taste and simmer over a fairly low heat while you cook the pasta.

**3** Bring a large pan of lightly salted water to the boil and cook the pasta until it is *al dente*. Drain the pasta and tip it into a large warmed serving bowl. Pour the caponata on top, and serve immediately, tossing the mixture well at the table.

### Cook's Tip
*It is worth buying genuine balsamic vinegar for this dish, as it has a unique sweet-sour flavour. If you can't find it, use a good-quality red wine vinegar.*

# Vegetable & Macaroni Bake

A tasty change from macaroni cheese, this recipe is delicious served with steamed fresh vegetables.

**Serves 6**

225g/8oz/2 cups wholemeal (whole-wheat) macaroni
225g/8oz leeks, sliced
45ml/3 tbsp Vegetable Stock
225g/8oz broccoli florets
50g/2oz/4 tbsp butter
50g/2oz/ $^1/_2$ cup plain (all-purpose) wholemeal (whole-wheat) flour
900ml/1 $^1/_2$ pints/3 $^3/_4$ cups milk
150g/5oz/1 $^1/_4$ cups grated mature (sharp) Cheddar cheese
5ml/1 tsp prepared English (hot) mustard
350g/12oz can sweetcorn kernels, drained
25g/1oz/ $^1/_2$ cup fresh wholemeal (whole-wheat) breadcrumbs
30ml/2 tbsp chopped fresh parsley
2 tomatoes, cut into 8 wedges
salt and freshly ground black pepper

**1** Preheat the oven to 200°C/400°F/Gas 6. Bring a pan of lightly salted water to the boil. Cook the macaroni until *al dente*.

**2** Meanwhile, combine the leeks and stock in a small pan. Cover and cook for about 10 minutes, until the leeks are tender.

**3** Bring a small pan of water to the boil and blanch the broccoli for 2 minutes. Drain the pasta, then the leeks and broccoli.

**4** Melt the butter in a large pan, stir in the flour and cook for 1–2 minutes, stirring constantly. Gradually add the milk, stirring constantly until the sauce boils and thickens.

**5** Remove the pan from the heat, add 115g/4oz/1 cup of the grated cheese and stir until it has melted. Stir in the pasta, leeks, broccoli, mustard and sweetcorn. Season to taste with salt and pepper and mix thoroughly. Transfer the mixture to an ovenproof dish.

**6** Mix the remaining cheese, breadcrumbs and parsley together, and sprinkle over the surface. Arrange the tomatoes on top and then bake for 30–40 minutes, until golden brown and bubbling.

# Spinach & Ricotta Conchiglione

Few pasta fillings are more pleasing than this mixture of chopped spinach and ricotta.

**Serves 4**

350g/12oz dried conchiglione
450ml/ ¾ pint/scant
    2 cups passata (bottled
    strained tomatoes)
275g/10oz frozen chopped
    spinach, thawed
50g/2oz white bread, crusts
    removed, crumbled
120ml/4fl oz/ ½ cup milk
60ml/4 tbsp olive oil
250g/9oz/1 ½ cups
    ricotta cheese
pinch of freshly grated nutmeg
1 garlic clove, crushed
2.5ml/ ½ tsp black olive
    paste (optional)
25g/1oz/ ⅓ cup freshly grated
    Parmesan cheese
25g/1oz/ ⅓ cup pine nuts
salt and freshly ground
    black pepper

**1** Bring a large pan of lightly salted water to the boil and cook the pasta until *al dente*. Drain, refresh under cold water, drain again and reserve until needed.

**2** Pour the passata into a nylon sieve placed over a bowl. Place the spinach in another sieve and press out any excess liquid with the back of a spoon.

**3** Place the bread, milk and 45ml/3 tbsp of the oil in a food processor and process to combine. Add the spinach and ricotta, and season with salt, pepper and nutmeg. Process briefly to mix.

**4** Discard the liquid that has drained from the passata. Tip the thicker liquid that remains in the sieve into a clean bowl and stir in the garlic, remaining oil and olive paste, if using. Spread this mixture evenly over the base of an ovenproof dish.

**5** Preheat the oven to 180°C/350°F/Gas 4. Spoon the spinach mixture into the conchiglione. Arrange them over the sauce and cover the dish with foil.

**6** Bake for about 15 minutes, until the pasta and sauce are both hot. Remove the foil, sprinkle with Parmesan cheese and pine nuts, and brown under a hot grill (broiler).

# Home-made Ravioli

It is a pleasure to make your own fresh pasta by hand.

**Serves 4–6**

200g/7oz/1¾ cups strong
    plain (all-purpose) bread flour
5ml/ ½ tsp salt
15ml/1 tbsp olive oil
2 eggs, beaten
melted butter, to serve
fresh basil, to garnish

**For the filling**
15ml/1 tbsp olive oil
1 small red onion, finely chopped
1 small green (bell) pepper,
    seeded and finely chopped
1 carrot, coarsely grated
50g/2oz/ ½ cup
    walnuts, chopped
115g/4oz/ ½ cup ricotta cheese
30ml/2 tbsp freshly grated
    Parmesan or Pecorino cheese,
    plus extra to serve
15ml/1 tbsp chopped fresh
    marjoram or basil
salt and freshly ground
    black pepper

**1** Make the filling. Heat the oil in a small pan and fry the onion, pepper and carrot for 5 minutes, then leave to cool. Mix with the walnuts, cheeses, marjoram or basil and seasoning.

**2** Place the flour, salt, oil and eggs in a food processor. Pulse to combine. Transfer the dough to a floured surface and knead for 5 minutes. Wrap in clear film (plastic wrap) and leave to rest for 20 minutes.

**3** Divide the dough in half and roll out each piece on a floured surface to 2.5mm/ ⅛in thick. Working with one piece at a time, fold it into three and re-roll. Repeat up to six times.

**4** Keep the rolled dough under clean, dry dishtowels while you fold and roll the second piece. Place small scoops of the filling in neat rows about 5cm/2in apart on the surface. Brush in between with a little water and then place the first pasta sheet on the top. Press down well between the rows then, using a ravioli or pastry cutter, cut into squares.

**5** Bring a large pan of lightly salted water to the boil and cook the ravioli, in batches if necessary, for 4–5 minutes. Drain well. Toss in a little melted butter. Serve with extra cheese and basil.

# Coriander Ravioli with Pumpkin Filling

A stunning herb pasta with a superb creamy pumpkin and roast garlic filling.

**Serves 4–6**
200g/7oz/1¾ cups strong
    unbleached white bread flour
2 eggs, beaten
pinch of salt
45ml/3 tbsp chopped fresh
    coriander (cilantro)
coriander (cilantro) sprigs and
    crushed coriander seeds,
    to garnish

**For the filling**
4 garlic cloves, unpeeled
450g/1lb pumpkin, peeled and
    seeds removed
115g/4oz/⅔ cup ricotta cheese
4 pieces of drained sun-dried
    tomatoes in oil, finely chopped,
    plus 30ml/2 tbsp of the oil
    from the jar
freshly ground black pepper

**1** Preheat the oven to 200°C/400°F/Gas 6. Place the flour, eggs, salt and coriander in a food processor. Pulse to combine. Knead the dough on a floured board for 5 minutes. Wrap in clear film (plastic wrap) and leave to rest for 20 minutes.

**2** Put the garlic on a baking sheet and bake for 10–15 minutes, until softened. Steam the pumpkin for 5–8 minutes until tender. Drain well and put in a bowl. Pop the garlic cloves out of their skins and mash them into the pumpkin with the ricotta and sun-dried tomatoes. Season with pepper.

**3** Divide the pasta into four pieces and flatten slightly. Using a pasta machine, on its thinnest setting, roll out each piece. Leave the sheets of pasta on a clean dishtowel. Using a 7.5cm/3in crinkle-edged round cutter, stamp out 36 rounds. Top 18 of the rounds with a teaspoonful of filling, brush the edges with water and place another round of pasta on top. Press to seal.

**4** Bring a large pan of water to the boil and cook the ravioli for 4–5 minutes. Drain and tip into a bowl. Add the tomato oil and toss gently. Garnish with the coriander sprigs and seeds.

# Ravioli with Cheese & Herbs

Home-made ravioli can be slightly fiddly, but they are well worth the effort.

semolina, to coat
75g/3oz/6 tbsp butter, melted,
    to serve

**Serves 4–6**
200g/7oz/1¾ cups strong
    unbleached white bread flour
2 eggs, beaten
pinch of salt

**For the filling**
225g/8oz/1 cup full-fat
    soft cheese
1 garlic clove, crushed
90ml/6 tbsp chopped fresh herbs

**1** Place the flour, eggs and salt in a food processor. Pulse to combine, then transfer the dough to a lightly floured surface and knead for 5 minutes, until smooth.

**2** Divide the dough into four pieces and flatten slightly. Using a pasta machine, on its thinnest setting, roll out each piece. Leave the sheets on clean dishtowels to dry slightly.

**3** Meanwhile, make the filling. Mix the soft cheese with the garlic and 60ml/4 tbsp of the herbs. Season to taste.

**4** Place small scoops of the filling on one of the pasta sheets, keeping them in neat rows, about 4cm/1½in apart. Brush the pasta with water, place another sheet on top and press down around each scoop of filling. Cut out the ravioli, toss them in semolina and leave to rest for 15 minutes. Make more ravioli in the same way.

**5** Bring a large pan of lightly salted water to the boil and cook the ravioli, in batches, for 4–5 minutes. Drain and toss with the melted butter. Sprinkle with the remaining herbs and serve.

> **Variation**
> Fill the ravioli with a mixture of full-fat soft cheese and crumbled Gorgonzola; omit the garlic and herbs. Sprinkle the cooked ravioli with toasted pine nuts.

# Sardinian Ravioli

Known as *culurgiones*, these ravioli, with their unusual mashed potato and mint filling, are from northern Sardinia. Here, they are gratinéed in the oven with butter and cheese, but they are often served dressed with a tomato sauce.

**Serves 4–6**
300g/11oz/2¾ cups strong
    white bread flour
3 eggs, beaten
5ml/1 tsp salt
50g/2oz/¼ cup butter
50g/2oz/⅔ cup freshly grated
    Pecorino cheese

*For the filling*
2 potatoes, each about 200g/
    7oz, diced
65g/2½oz/generous ⅔ cup
    freshly grated hard salty
    Pecorino cheese
75g/3oz soft fresh
    Pecorino cheese
1 egg yolk
1 large bunch fresh mint, leaves
    removed and chopped
good pinch of saffron powder
salt and freshly ground
    black pepper

**1** First, make the filling. Cook the potatoes in salted boiling water for 15–20 minutes, or until soft. Drain the potatoes and tip into a bowl, then mash until smooth. Leave until cold.

**2** Add both the cheeses, the egg yolk, mint and saffron to the mashed potatoes and season with salt and pepper to taste. Stir well to mix.

**3** Place the flour, eggs and salt in a food processor. Pulse to combine, then transfer the dough to a lightly floured surface and knead for 5 minutes, until smooth.

**4** Using a pasta machine, roll out one-quarter of the pasta into a 90cm–1 metre/36–39in strip. Cut the strip with a sharp knife into 2 × 45–50cm/18–20in lengths.

**5** With a fluted 10cm/4in biscuit (cookie) cutter, cut out four to five discs from one of the pasta strips. Put a mound of filling on one side of each disc. Brush the edges with water, then fold the dough over the filling to make what looks like a small turnover. Pleat the curved edge on each ravioli to seal.

**6** Put the ravioli on floured dishtowels, sprinkle with flour and leave to dry. Repeat the process to make more ravioli.

**7** Preheat the oven to 190°C/375°F/Gas 5. Bring a large pan of lightly salted water to the boil and cook the ravioli, in batches if necessary, for 4–5 minutes. Meanwhile, melt the butter in a small pan.

**8** Drain the ravioli, tip them into a large ovenproof dish and pour the melted butter over them. Sprinkle with the grated Pecorino and bake in the oven for 10–15 minutes, until golden and bubbly. Allow to stand for 5 minutes before serving.

# Tortelli with Squash Stuffing

Winter squash come in all shapes and sizes. Some, like Munchkins and Mama Mia, have delectable flesh, which tastes great with pasta.

**Serves 4–6**
300g/11oz/2¾ cups strong
    white bread flour
3 eggs, beaten
5ml/1 tsp salt
melted butter and freshly grated
    Parmesan cheese, to serve

*For the filling*
1kg/2¼ lb winter squash (weight
    with shell)
75g/3oz/1½ cups amaretti,
    crushed
2 eggs, beaten
75g/3oz/1 cup freshly grated
    Parmesan cheese
pinch of freshly grated nutmeg
fresh white breadcrumbs
    (optional)
salt and freshly ground
    black pepper

**1** Preheat the oven to 190°C/375°F/Gas 5. Make the filling. Cut the squash into wedges, leaving the skin on. Place these in a roasting pan, cover and bake for 30–45 minutes, until soft. Scoop the flesh into a food processor and process until smooth.

**2** Scrape the squash purée into a bowl and add the amaretti crumbs, eggs, Parmesan and nutmeg. Season with salt and pepper. If the mixture is too sloppy, add 15–30ml/1–2 tbsp of the breadcrumbs. Set aside.

**3** Place the flour, eggs and salt in the clean food processor. Pulse to combine, then transfer the dough to a lightly floured surface and knead for 5 minutes. Roll it out very thinly, by hand or in a pasta machine.

**4** Place tablespoons of filling every 6cm/2½in along a sheet of pasta in rows 5cm/2in apart. Moisten. Cover with another sheet and press down gently. Use a fluted pastry wheel to cut between the rows to form rectangles. Leave to dry for 30 minutes.

**5** Bring a large pan of lightly salted water to the boil and cook the tortelli, in batches, for 4–5 minutes. Drain and place in warmed dishes. Spoon the melted butter over, sprinkle with Parmesan and serve immediately.

# Agnolotti with Taleggio & Marjoram

The filling for these little half-moons is very simple, but the combination of flavours is delicious.

**Serves 6–8**

300g/11oz/2¾ cups strong white bread flour
3 eggs, beaten
5ml/1 tsp salt

350–400g/12–14oz
 Taleggio cheese
about 30ml/2 tbsp finely chopped
 fresh marjoram, plus extra
 to garnish
salt and freshly ground
 black pepper
115g/4oz/½ cup hot melted
 butter and freshly grated
 Parmesan cheese, to serve

**1** Place the flour, eggs and salt in a food processor. Pulse to combine. Transfer the dough to a floured surface and knead for 5 minutes, until smooth. Using a pasta machine, roll out one-quarter of the dough into a strip 90cm–1metre/36–39in long. Cut the strip into 2 × 45–50cm/18–20in lengths.

**2** Cut eight to ten little cubes of Taleggio and space them evenly along one side of one of the pasta strips. Sprinkle each Taleggio cube with chopped marjoram and pepper to taste. Brush a little water around each cube of cheese, then fold the plain side of the pasta strip over them.

**3** Starting from the folded edge, press gently around each cube with your fingertips, pushing the air out. Sprinkle lightly with flour. Using half of a 5cm/2in fluted round ravioli or biscuit (cookie) cutter, cut around each cube to make a half-moon shape. The folded edge should be the straight edge.

**4** Put the agnolotti on floured dishtowels, sprinkle lightly with flour and leave to dry while making more agnolotti.

**5** Bring a large pan of lightly salted water to the boil and cook the agnolotti until *al dente*.

**6** Drain the agnolotti and divide them equally among six to eight warmed individual bowls. Drizzle sizzling hot butter over them and sprinkle with Parmesan and marjoram. Hand around more grated Parmesan separately.

# Pansotti with Herbs & Cheese

Pasta triangles with a ricotta and herb filling, pansotti taste wonderful with a walnut sauce.

**Serves 6–8**

300g/11oz/2¾ cups strong white bread flour
3 eggs, beaten
5ml/1 tsp salt
25g/1oz/1 cup chopped fresh herbs
115g/4oz/½ cup hot melted butter and freshly grated Parmesan cheese, to serve

**For the filling**
250g/9oz/generous 1 cup ricotta cheese
150g/5oz/1½ cups freshly grated Parmesan cheese

1 large handful fresh basil leaves,
 finely chopped
1 large handful fresh flat leaf
 parsley, finely chopped
a few sprigs fresh marjoram or
 oregano, leaves removed and
 finely chopped
1 garlic clove, crushed
1 small egg
salt and freshly ground
 black pepper

**For the sauce**
115g/4oz/1 cup walnuts
1 garlic clove, halved
60ml/4 tbsp extra virgin olive oil
120ml/4fl oz/½ cup double
 (heavy) cream

**1** Place the flour, eggs, salt and herbs in a food processor. Pulse to combine, then transfer the dough to a lightly floured surface and knead for 5 minutes, until smooth.

**2** Make the filling. Mash the ricotta in a bowl. Add the grated Parmesan, herbs, garlic and egg and beat well. Season to taste.

**3** Make the sauce. Put the walnuts, garlic and oil in a food processor, and process to a paste, then add up to 120ml/4fl oz/½ cup warm water through the feeder tube to slacken the consistency. Spoon the mixture into a large bowl and beat in the cream.

**4** Using a pasta machine, roll out one-quarter of the pasta into a 90cm–1metre/36–39in strip. Cut the strip with a sharp knife into 2 × 45–50cm/18–20in lengths.

**5** Using a 5cm/2in square ravioli cutter, cut eight to ten squares from one of the pasta strips. Put a mound of filling in the centre of each square. Brush a little water around the edge of the dough, then fold each square diagonally in half over the filling to make a triangle. Press gently to seal.

**6** Spread out the pansotti on clean floured dishtowels, sprinkle lightly with flour and leave to dry. Make more pansotti in the same way. Gently reheat the remaining walnut sauce.

**7** Bring a large pan of lightly salted water to the boil and cook the pansotti until *al dente*. Meanwhile, add a ladleful of the pasta cooking water to the walnut sauce to thin it down.

**8** Drain the pansotti and tip them into the bowl of walnut sauce. Drizzle the hot melted butter over them, toss well, then sprinkle with grated Parmesan. Serve immediately, with more grated Parmesan handed separately.

# Baked Vegetable Lasagne

Vegetable lasagne became a bit of a cliché when restaurants began catering for vegetarians, but it can be a very tasty dish.

### Serves 8

30ml/2 tbsp olive oil
1 medium onion, finely chopped
500g/1¼lb tomatoes, chopped
75g/3oz/6 tbsp butter
675g/1½lb/8 cups wild
   mushrooms, sliced
2 garlic cloves, finely chopped
juice of ½ lemon
12–16 fresh lasagne sheets,
   precooked if necessary
175g/6oz/2 cups freshly grated
   Parmesan cheese
salt and freshly ground
   black pepper

### For the white sauce

50g/2oz/¼ cup butter
50g/2oz/½ cup plain (all-
   purpose) flour
900ml/1½ pints/3¾ cups
   hot milk

**1** Preheat the oven to 200°C/400°F/Gas 6. Heat the oil in a pan and sauté the onion until translucent. Add the tomatoes and cook for 6–8 minutes, stirring often. Season and set aside.

**2** Heat half the butter in a frying pan and cook the mushrooms until the juices run. Add the garlic, lemon juice and seasoning. Cook until the liquid has almost completely evaporated and the mushrooms are starting to brown. Set aside.

**3** Make the white sauce. Melt the butter in a pan, add the flour and cook, stirring constantly, for 1–2 minutes. Gradually add the hot milk, stirring until the sauce boils and thickens.

**4** Spread a spoonful of the white sauce over the base of an ovenproof dish and cover it with four sheets of lasagne. Add a thin layer of mushrooms, then a layer of white sauce. Sprinkle with a little Parmesan. Make another layer of pasta, spread with a thin layer of the tomato mixture, then add a layer of white sauce. Sprinkle with cheese. Repeat the layers, ending with a layer of pasta coated with white sauce, saving some cheese.

**5** Sprinkle with the remaining Parmesan cheese, dot with the remaining butter and bake for 20 minutes, until bubbling.

---

# Aubergine Lasagne

Aubergines are very satisfying vegetables and give substance to this tasty bake.

salt and freshly ground black pepper

**For the cheese sauce**
25g/1oz/2 tbsp butter
25g/1oz/¼ cup plain (all-purpose) flour
300ml/½ pint/1¼ cups milk
2.5ml/½ tsp prepared English (hot) mustard
115g/4oz/1 cup grated mature (sharp) Cheddar
15ml/1 tbsp freshly grated Parmesan cheese

**Serves 4**
3 medium aubergines (eggplants), sliced
75ml/5 tbsp olive oil
2 large onions, finely chopped
2 x 400g/14oz cans chopped tomatoes
5ml/1 tsp dried mixed herbs
2–3 garlic cloves, crushed
6 no-precook lasagne sheets

**1** Layer the aubergine slices in a colander, sprinkling each layer lightly with salt. Leave to stand for 30 minutes, then rinse well and pat dry with kitchen paper.

**2** Heat 60ml/4 tbsp of the oil in a large pan, fry the aubergine slices until soft and drain on kitchen paper. Add the remaining oil to the pan, cook the onions for 5 minutes, then stir in the tomatoes, herbs, garlic and seasoning. Bring to the boil, then cover the pan and simmer the mixture for 30 minutes.

**3** Meanwhile, make the cheese sauce. Melt the butter in a pan, stir in the flour and cook for 1–2 minutes, stirring constantly. Gradually add the milk, stirring until the sauce boils and thickens. Stir in the mustard, cheeses and seasoning.

**4** Preheat the oven to 200°C/400°F/Gas 6. Arrange half the aubergines in the base of a large ovenproof dish and spoon over half the tomato sauce. Arrange three sheets of lasagne on top. Make a second layer in the same way. Spoon over the cheese sauce and cover the dish with foil.

**5** Bake for 30 minutes. Remove the foil for the last 10 minutes. Leave to stand for 5–10 minutes before serving.

# Spinach, Walnut & Gruyère Lasagne

This nutty lasagne introduces a delicious combination of flavours.

salt and freshly ground black pepper
fresh parsley, to garnish

**Serves 8**
45ml/3 tbsp walnut oil
1 large onion, chopped
225g/8oz celeriac, finely chopped
1 large garlic clove, finely chopped
2.5ml/½ tsp granulated sugar
115g/4oz/1 cup chopped walnuts
300ml/½ pint/1¼ cups passata (bottled strained tomatoes)
150ml/¼ pint/⅔ cup Dubonnet
350g/12oz no-precook spinach lasagne sheets
30ml/2 tbsp chopped fresh basil

**For the spinach sauce**
75g/3oz/6 tbsp butter
30ml/2 tbsp walnut oil
1 medium onion, chopped
75g/3oz/¾ cup plain (all-purpose) flour
5ml/1 tsp dried mustard
1.2 litres/2 pints/5 cups milk
225g/8oz/2 cups grated Gruyère cheese
freshly grated nutmeg
450g/1lb frozen spinach, thawed and puréed

**1** Heat the oil in a heavy pan, add the onion and celeriac and sauté for 8–10 minutes. Add the garlic to the pan and cook for about 1 minute, then add the sugar, walnuts, passata and Dubonnet. Season to taste with salt and pepper. Simmer, uncovered, for 25 minutes.

**2** Make the spinach sauce. Melt the butter with the oil and cook the onion for 5 minutes. Stir in the flour and cook, stirring, for 1 minute, then add the mustard powder and milk, stirring vigorously until the sauce boils and thickens. Remove from the heat and stir in three-quarters of the Gruyère. Season with salt, pepper and nutmeg. Finally, stir in the spinach.

**3** Preheat the oven to 180°C/350°F/Gas 4. Spread a layer of the spinach sauce on the base of a large ovenproof dish. Top with a little walnut and tomato sauce, then add a layer of lasagne sheets. Continue until the dish is full, ending with a layer of either sauce. Sprinkle the remaining Gruyère over the top, followed by the basil. Bake for 45 minutes. Leave to stand for 5–10 minutes before serving, garnished with parsley.

# Lasagne Rolls

Just as tasty as ordinary vegetarian lasagne, the elegant presentation of this dish gives it added interest.

**Serves 4**
8–10 fresh lasagne sheets
225g/8oz fresh spinach
115g/4oz/1¾ cups
    mushrooms, sliced
⅓ quantity Lentil Bolognese
115g/4oz mozzarella cheese,
    thinly sliced
freshly grated Parmesan cheese

salt and freshly ground
    black pepper

**For the sauce**
40g/1½ oz/⅓ cup plain (all-
    purpose) flour
40g/1½ oz/3 tbsp butter
600ml/1 pint/2½ cups milk
freshly grated nutmeg

**1** Bring a large pan of lightly salted water to the boil and cook the lasagne until it is *al dente*. Drain and leave to cool.

**2** Cook the spinach, in just the water clinging to the leaves after washing, for 2 minutes over a low heat. Add the sliced mushrooms and cook, stirring occasionally, for a further 2 minutes. Drain very well, pressing out all the excess moisture, and chop roughly.

**3** Lay out the pasta sheets and spread with the lentil bolognese, spinach, mushrooms and mozzarella slices. Roll up each sheet and place in a single layer in a large ovenproof dish with the join down.

**4** To make the sauce, put the flour, butter and milk into a pan and gradually bring to the boil, whisking constantly until the sauce is thick and smooth. Lower the heat. Simmer for 2 minutes, then season with salt and pepper and stir in grated nutmeg to taste.

**5** Preheat the grill (broiler). Pour the sauce over the pasta, sprinkle over the grated Parmesan and brown under the grill. Serve immediately.

# Spirali with Sour Cream Sauce

Entertaining unexpected guests need never be a problem while you have easy recipes such as this one at your command.

**Serves 4**
350g/12oz/3 cups dried spirali
25g/1oz/2 tbsp butter
1 onion, chopped
1 garlic clove, chopped
15ml/1 tbsp chopped
    fresh oregano

300ml/½ pint/1¼ cups
    sour cream
75g/3oz/¾ cup grated
    mozzarella cheese
75g/3oz/¾ cup grated Bel
    Paese cheese
5 sun-dried tomatoes in oil,
    drained and sliced
salt and freshly ground
    black pepper

**1** Bring a large pan of lightly salted water to the boil and cook the pasta until it is *al dente*.

**2** Meanwhile, melt the butter in a large frying pan and fry the onion over a medium heat, stirring frequently, for 8 minutes, until softened. Add the garlic and cook for 1 minute.

**3** Stir in the oregano and sour cream, and heat gently until almost boiling. Stir in the mozzarella and Bel Paese and heat gently, stirring occasionally, until the cheeses have melted. Add the sliced sun-dried tomatoes and season to taste.

**4** Drain the pasta and tip it into a serving bowl. Pour over the sauce and toss well to coat. Serve immediately.

**Variation**
*Use leeks, shallots or an Italian white onion instead of an ordinary brown onion.*

# Lentil Bolognese

This is a really useful, tasty and nutritious sauce to serve with pasta.

**Serves 6**
45ml/3 tbsp olive oil
1 onion, chopped
2 garlic cloves, crushed
2 carrots, coarsely grated
2 celery sticks, chopped
115g/4oz/⅔ cup red lentils
115g/4oz can chopped tomatoes
30ml/2 tbsp tomato purée (paste)
450ml/¾ pint/scant 2 cups stock
15ml/1 tbsp fresh marjoram,
    chopped, or 5ml/1 tsp
    dried marjoram
salt and black pepper

**1** Heat the olive oil in a large, heavy pan. Add the onion, garlic, carrots and celery, and fry over a low heat, stirring occasionally, until soft.

**2** Stir in the lentils, tomatoes, tomato purée, stock and marjoram, season to taste and bring to the boil. Lower the heat, then simmer for 20 minutes until thick.

# Buckwheat Noodles with Goat's Cheese

The earthy flavour of buckwheat goes well with peppery rocket and creamy goat's cheese in this tasty supper dish.

**Serves 4**
75g/3oz/ ¾ cup hazelnuts
350g/12oz buckwheat noodles
50g/2oz/ ¼ cup butter
2 garlic cloves, finely chopped
4 shallots, sliced
a large handful of rocket
 (arugula) leaves
175g/6oz goat's cheese
salt and freshly ground
 black pepper

**1** Preheat the grill (broiler). Spread out the hazelnuts in the grill pan and place them under a medium heat until they are golden brown. Watch them closely, as they tend to burn easily. Tip the nuts into a clean dishtowel and rub off the skins. Set aside.

**2** Bring a large pan of lightly salted water to the boil and cook the noodles until they are just tender. Drain well.

**3** Heat the butter in a large, heavy frying pan. Add the garlic and shallots, and cook over a medium heat, stirring constantly, for 2–3 minutes, until the shallots are soft.

**4** Add the hazelnuts and fry, stirring constantly, for about 1 minute. Add the rocket leaves and, when they are just starting to wilt, toss in the noodles and heat them through. Season with salt and pepper to taste. Crumble in the goat's cheese and serve immediately.

> **Variations**
> • Substitute watercress or spinach for the rocket (arugula).
> • You could use fresh wholemeal (whole-wheat) noodles instead of the buckwheat noodles.

# Indian Mee Goreng

This is a truly international dish combining a mixture of traditional Indian, Chinese and Western ingredients.

**Serves 4–6**
450g/1lb fresh yellow egg noodles
60–90ml/4–6 tbsp vegetable oil
150g/5oz firm beancurd
 (tofu), cubed
2 eggs
30ml/2 tbsp water
1 onion, sliced
1 garlic clove, crushed
15ml/1 tbsp light soy sauce
30–45ml/2–3 tbsp
 tomato ketchup
15ml/1 tbsp chilli sauce, or
 to taste
1 large cooked potato, diced
4 spring onions
 (scallions), shredded
1–2 fresh green chillies, seeded
 and thinly sliced
salt and freshly ground
 black pepper

**1** Bring a large pan of lightly salted water to the boil and cook the fresh egg noodles for just 2 minutes. Drain, rinse under cold water, drain again and set aside.

**2** Heat 30ml/2 tbsp of the oil in a large, heavy frying pan. Add the beancurd and fry the cubes over a medium heat until golden brown. Lift them out with a slotted spoon and set aside.

**3** In a bowl, beat the eggs with the water and add a little salt and pepper. Pour the mixture into the oil remaining in the frying pan and make an omelette. Flip over, cook the other side, then slide the omelette out of the pan. Blot the surface with kitchen paper, roll it up and slice it thinly.

**4** Preheat a wok. Swirl in the remaining oil, and stir-fry the onion and garlic for 2–3 minutes. Add the drained noodles, soy sauce, ketchup and chilli sauce. Toss well over a medium heat for 2 minutes, then add the diced potato. Reserve a few spring onions for the garnish and stir the rest into the noodles with the chillies and the beancurd.

**5** When the mixture is piping hot, stir in the omelette strips. Transfer to a warmed platter, garnish with the remaining spring onions and serve immediately.

# Somen Noodles with Saffron Sauce

It is unusual to find somen noodles teamed with asparagus, but the partnership works remarkably well.

**Serves 4**
450g/1lb young asparagus
pinch of saffron threads
30ml/2 tbsp boiling water
25g/1oz/2 tbsp butter
2 shallots, finely chopped
30ml/2 tbsp white wine
250ml/8fl oz/1 cup double
   (heavy) cream
grated rind and juice of ½ lemon
115g/4oz/1 cup peas
350g/12oz dried somen noodles
½ bunch fresh chervil,
   roughly chopped
salt and freshly ground
   black pepper

**1** Cut off the asparagus tips, then slice the remaining spears into short rounds. Steep the saffron in the boiling water in a cup or small bowl.

**2** Melt the butter in a pan, add the shallots and cook over a low heat, stirring occasionally, for 3 minutes, until soft.

**3** Stir in the white wine, cream and steeped saffron. Bring to the boil, lower the heat and simmer gently for 5 minutes, or until the sauce thickens to a coating consistency. Add the grated lemon rind and juice and season with salt and pepper to taste.

**4** Bring a large pan of lightly salted water to the boil. Cook the asparagus tips for 2 minutes, scoop them out with a slotted spoon and add them to the sauce.

**5** Cook the peas and asparagus rounds in the boiling water until just tender. Scoop them out and add them to the sauce.

**6** Let the water return to the boil and cook the somen noodles until just tender. Drain, return to the clean pan and pour the sauce over the top.

**7** Toss the noodles with the sauce and vegetables, adding the chervil and more salt and pepper if needed. Serve immediately, on warmed plates.

# Fried Noodles with Beansprouts & Asparagus

Soft fried noodles contrast beautifully with crisp beansprouts and asparagus.

**Serves 2**
115g/4oz dried egg noodles
60ml/4 tbsp vegetable oil
1 small onion, chopped
2.5cm/1in piece of fresh root
   ginger, peeled and grated
2 garlic cloves, crushed
175g/6oz young
   asparagus, trimmed
115g/4oz/2 cups beansprouts
4 spring onions (scallions), sliced
45ml/3 tbsp soy sauce
salt and freshly ground
   black pepper

**1** Bring a large pan of lightly salted water to the boil and cook the noodles briefly until they are just tender. Drain and toss in 30ml/2 tbsp of the oil.

**2** Preheat a wok, add the remaining oil and swirl it around. When it is very hot, add the onion, ginger and garlic and stir-fry over a medium heat for 2–3 minutes. Add the asparagus and stir-fry for 2–3 minutes more.

**3** Add the noodles and beansprouts and stir-fry for 2 minutes, then stir in the spring onions and soy sauce. Season with salt and pepper, if necessary, stir-fry for 1 minute, then transfer to a warmed bowl. Serve immediately.

---

**Cook's Tip**

*The beansprouts on sale in supermarkets and Chinese food stores are usually those of mung beans. However, the sprouts of a wide variety of beans, peas and seeds are also edible and can be home-grown in a large jar or a special sprouter. Aduki beans, chickpeas, green or brown lentils, soya beans, alfalfa seeds, sesame seeds, pumpkin seeds and sunflower seeds are all suitable for sprouting. Store fresh sprouts in a covered container in the refrigerator for up to 1 week.*

# Types of Pasta

The first forms of pasta were thin strings or ribbons, but it wasn't long before people started experimenting with shapes. Soon there were hundreds of these, often starting out as regional specialities, but spreading to the wider world. Today the range is enormous, and continues to grow. Shapes range from the beautiful to the bizarre. This book introduces a wide selection, but there's no need to limit yourself to our suggestions. Feel free to make substitutions, but bear in mind that long strands work best with thinner sauces, while short shapes are good with chunky sauces. Choose tubes or shells if you want to trap the sauce inside. Remember, too, that pasta names often vary from region to region.

## Long Pasta

**Bucatini** looks like chunky spaghetti, but is hollow. **Bucatoni** is a fatter version, while **perciatelli** is bucatini by another name.

**Capelli** or **capelli d'angelo** translates as angel hair pasta, which is a fanciful name for this superfine pasta. It is often packed in nests – **capelli d'angelo a nidi. Capellini** are similar strands.

**Chitarra** is a square-shaped form of spaghetti, so named because it is made on a frame that resembles a guitar.

**Fusilli lunghi,** also known as **fusilli col buco,** are long twisted strands or spirals.

**Linguine** are slim ribbons. The name means "little tongues". This popular form of pasta is very good for serving with creamy coating sauces.

**Macaroni (maccheroni),** tubular pasta, was one of the first shapes to be made, and remains very popular. Two short forms, the curved elbow macaroni and short-cut macaroni, are particularly widely used. A thin form of the long strands is **maccheroncini.**

**Pappardelle** are broad ribbon noodles, with either plain or wavy edges. **Trenette** are similar.

**Spaghetti** needs no introduction, but do try the less familiar forms, such as the skinny **spaghettini** or the flavoured **spaghetti con spinaci** (with spinach) or **spaghetti integrali** (whole-wheat).

**Strangozzi** is a thin noodle that is often sold as a loose plait (braid). The basil flavour is delicious.

**Tagliatelle** is the most common form of ribbon noodle. It is sold in nests, which unravel on cooking. Several flavours are available, a popular mix being **paglia e fieno** (straw and hay) which consists of separate nests of egg noodles and spinach-flavoured noodles. The Roman version of tagliatelle is called **fettuccine. Tagliolini, tagliarini** and **fidelini** are thin ribbon noodles.

**Vermicelli** is very fine spaghetti.

**Ziti** is very long, thick and tubular, like macaroni, and is often broken into shorter lengths before being cooked.

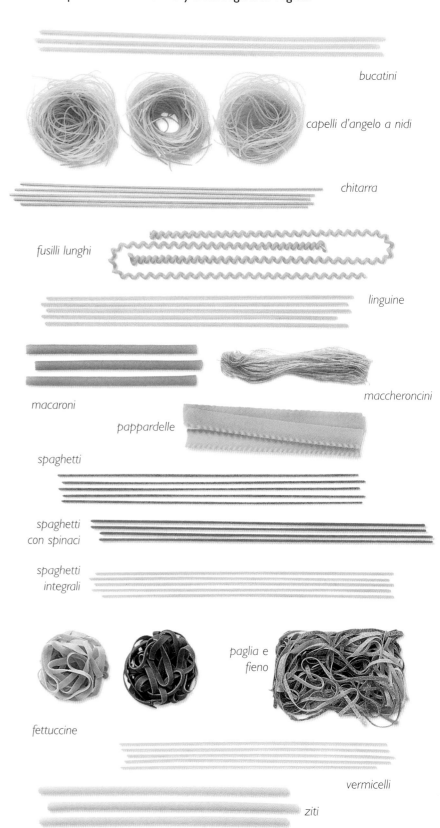

bucatini

capelli d'angelo a nidi

chitarra

fusilli lunghi

linguine

macaroni

maccheroncini

pappardelle

spaghetti

spaghetti con spinaci

spaghetti integrali

paglia e fieno

fettuccine

vermicelli

ziti

## Short Pasta (Shapes)

**Conchiglie** are shells. Perfect for trapping sauces, they come in various sizes, from tiny **conchigliette** for soups to **conchiglione**, the jumbo shells which can be stuffed.

**Eliche** are among several spiral-shaped pastas and resemble **fusilli** and **spirali** (which tend to be more open). They come in various thicknesses and flavours.

**Farfalle** are known in English as butterflies or bow-ties, which they resemble. They look very pretty on the plate, and are so popular that manufacturers produce several different varieties, including the ever-popular **farfalle tricolore**, which mixes plain or ridged red, green and yellow shapes.

**Fiorelli** are very pretty designer shapes that look rather like oyster mushrooms, with frilly edges. They are not unlike the bell-shaped **campanelle**.

**Fusilli** are spirals, formed by winding fresh dough around a thin rod. They tend to relax and unwind a little when placed in boiling water.

**Garganelli** are a regional form of penne. Short and tubular, they look a little like scrolls, thanks to the special tool on which they are rolled. Called *il pettine*, this resembles a large comb.

**Orecchiette** are endearing small shapes, so named because they look like little ears. They are slightly chewy and are served with robust sauces.

**Penne** or quills are short lengths of tubular pasta which are cut on the slant so their ends are pointed. Sturdy and capable of holding sauces inside their hollow centres, they are deservedly popular. Both plain – **penne lisce** – and ridged versions – **penne rigate** – are available. **Rigatoni** are straight ridged tubes, somewhat fatter than penne.

**Pipe** are small pasta shapes. They don't look much like pipes, which is the translation of their Italian name, but rather resemble small shells. **Pipe rigate** is the ridged version. They are available plain and whole-wheat.

**Ruote** or **Rotelle** are small wagon wheel shapes. They come in various flavours and colours and are popular with children.

**Strozzapreti** sounds like such a pretty name. The word, however, means "priest stranglers", which is somewhat less attractive! Legend has it that the priest who originally tried them ate far too many and almost choked to death. Each shape consists of two slim strands of pasta that are twisted or "strangled" together.

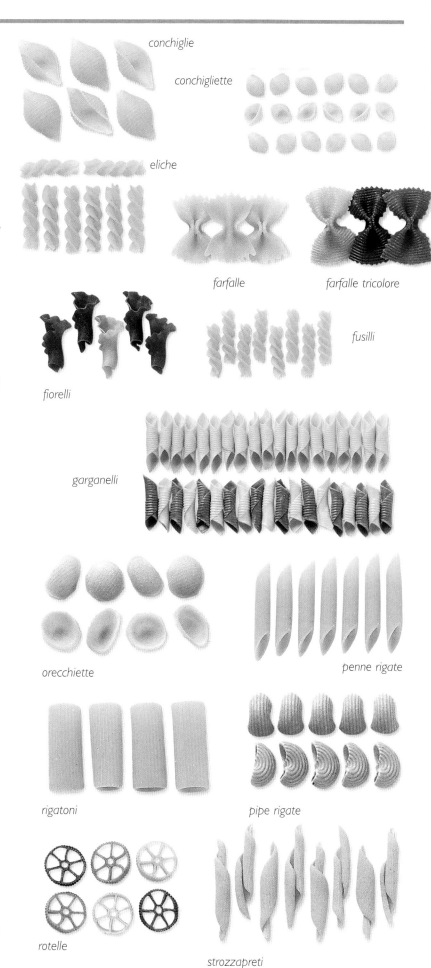

*conchiglie*

*conchigliette*

*eliche*

*farfalle*

*farfalle tricolore*

*fusilli*

*fiorelli*

*garganelli*

*orecchiette*

*penne rigate*

*rigatoni*

*pipe rigate*

*rotelle*

*strozzapreti*

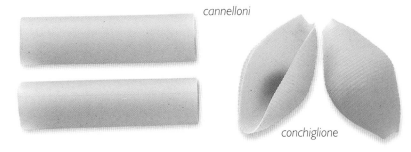

*cannelloni*

*conchiglione*

*lasagne*

*lasagne verdi*

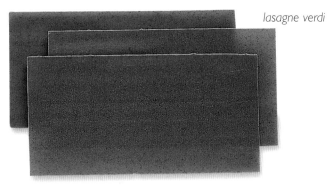

*lasagnette*

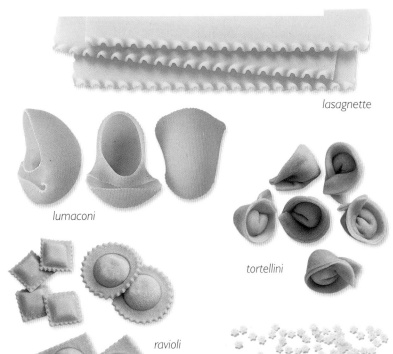

*lumaconi*

*tortellini*

*ravioli*

*stellette*

*tubetti*

## Pasta for Stuffing and Layering

**Cannelloni** About 10cm/4in in length, these large tubes are stuffed, coated in sauce and baked in the oven. In Italy, cannelloni are traditionally made by rolling fresh lasagne sheets around the filling, but the dried tubes are more convenient. Either pipe the filling in with a piping (pastry) bag, or use a teaspoon.

**Conchiglione** Jumbo pasta shells, these are wonderful for stuffing and look very pretty. They come in plain, spinach and tomato flavours, both smooth and ridged.

**Lasagne** This popular form of pasta comes in flat or wavy sheets, pre-cut for layering, and can be fresh or dried. There is also a no-precook version, which is very convenient, as it needs only to be layered with the sauce or sauces and cooks as the dish bakes in the oven. There are some drawbacks with no-precook pasta – purists say it doesn't compare with other types in terms of taste, but as long as you buy a quality pasta, use more sauce than usual and cook the lasagne for at least 45 minutes, it gives a very good result. Sizes vary, so when you find one that fits your lasagne dish perfectly, it is well worth making a note of the manufacturer. You can snap sheets to fit, but they seldom break where you want them to. If you choose fresh or regular dried pasta, you will need to cook it before layering. Follow the instructions on the packet.

**Flavoured lasagne** Lasagne comes in several flavours, including green (spinach), brown (whole-wheat) and two tones of yellow, one being the plain lasagne and the other being the version with added egg.

**Lasagnette** are long, narrow strips of flat pasta, which are crimped on one or two sides. They are used in the same way as lasagne sheets.

**Lumaconi** These look a bit like large snail shells, with an opening at either end. They are fiddly to stuff, but make an interesting change from more common shapes.

### Filled Pasta
Fresh and dried filled pasta shapes are available. The range includes **ravioli** and **tortellini**, both of which can be served quite simply, with melted butter or a light sauce, and the lesser-known **agnolotti**, which are half-moon shaped, like miniature turnovers.

### Pastina
These are miniature shapes, usually served in broth or soup. There are dozens of varieties, including **tubetti**, **stellette**, **risoni**, **peperini**, **ditalini** and **fregola**, which resembles couscous.

# Types of Noodle

Asian noodles are usually made from wheat, as is Italian pasta, but may also be made from rice, buckwheat, arrowroot or mung beans. The noodles are formed by various methods, the most dramatic of which is when the cook hurls pieces of dough into the air, twirling and twisting until they stretch and lengthen to form long, thin strands. In principle, the process is similar to that adopted by chefs when shaping pizza dough, but is even more impressive. There are many different types of noodle, some of which must be soaked in warm water before being cooked briefly – or just heated – in boiling water. Check the instructions on the packet, as timings can vary widely, but in general, the thinner the noodle, the less cooking it will need. In addition to being boiled, or heated in soups, noodles are an integral part of many vegetable dishes, and are often stir-fried or deep-fried. They may need to be boiled or soaked, then well drained, before frying.

**Cellophane Noodles** are made from ground mung beans, and are also known as bean thread, transparent or glass noodles. Although very thin, the strands are firm and resilient and stay that way when cooked, never becoming soggy. Cellophane noodles are not served solo, but are added to soups or braised dishes.

**Egg Noodles** These can be fresh or dried, and come in various thicknesses, including fine, medium and broad. They are often packed in what look like skeins or coils, and the general rule is to use one of these per person. The Japanese equivalent are called **ramen**.

**Rice Noodles** come in several different forms and are usually sold in bundles. The very thin white ones are called **rice vermicelli**. These cook almost instantly when added to hot broth, provided they have first been soaked in warm water.

**Soba Noodles** Japanese buckwheat noodles, these often include wheat flour and/or yam flour. They are much darker in colour than regular wheat noodles and are sold in bundles.

**Somen Noodles** also come from Japan, and are made from wheat starch. Thin and delicate, they are sold in bundles fastened with a paper band.

**Udon Noodles** are plain wheat noodles from Japan. They are available fresh, precooked or dried.

---

**Noodle Know-how**
*•Store dried noodles in airtight boxes, and store fresh noodles in the refrigerator, having checked the use-by date on the packaging.*
*•As a general rule, allow 75–115g/3–4oz noodles per person.*
*•Many recipes call for noodles to be soaked in warm water before being cooked; check the recipe, as you need to allow the requisite time.*
*•It is easy to overcook noodles. Remove them from the heat when they are barely tender and drain them in a colander. If you are not using them immediately, rinse them under cold running water so they stop cooking, then drain them again.*
*•If you are going to fry the prepared noodles, it is a good idea to blot them dry with kitchen paper.*

cellophane noodles

egg noodles

rice noodles

soba noodles

somen noodles

udon noodles

# Techniques

## Basic Pasta Dough

Making pasta dough at home isn't difficult, especially if you use a food processor and a pasta machine. If you have neither, make the pasta by hand. It may not end up quite as thin as you would like, but it will still taste delicious. For enough pasta to serve three to four people, you will need 200g/7oz/1¾ cups plain (all-purpose) white flour, a pinch of salt, 2 eggs and 15ml/1 tbsp olive oil. You can also use strong white bread flour. If you are going to make flavoured pasta (see below), the quantities may need to be slightly changed.

### To make the dough by hand

**I** To make the dough by hand, sift the flour and salt into a heap on a clean work surface and make a well in the centre with your fist.

**2** Lightly beat the eggs with the oil and pour into the well. Mix the egg mixture into the flour with your fingers. Alternatively, add the eggs and oil to the well and beat lightly with a fork, gradually drawing in the flour.

**3** Knead the pasta until smooth, wrap it and set it aside to rest for at least 30 minutes before rolling it out. It will be much more elastic after resting.

### To make the dough in a food processor

**I** Sift the flour into the bowl of a food processor and add the salt.

**2** Lightly beat the eggs with the oil and pour them in, together with any chosen flavouring. Process until the dough begins to come together, then tip it out and knead it until smooth. Wrap and rest for 40 minutes before shaping.

### Variations

*Tomato Pasta* Add 30ml/2 tbsp tomato purée (paste) to the flour and use only 1½ eggs.
*Herb Pasta* Add 45ml/3 tbsp chopped fresh herbs to the flour.
*Wholemeal Pasta* Use 150g/5oz/1¼ cups wholemeal (whole-wheat) flour sifted with 25g/1oz/¼ cup plain (all-purpose) white flour.
*Spinach Pasta* Cook 150g/5oz frozen leaf spinach, squeeze out the moisture, then blend with 2 eggs. Make as above, but use a little extra flour.

### To shape the dough in a pasta machine

**I** Feed it several times through the machine, using the highest setting first, then reducing the setting until the required thickness is achieved.

**2** Fit the special cutter and turn the handle if you want to produce fettuccine or tagliatelle. A narrower cutter will produce spaghetti or tagliarini. Toss the pasta lightly in flour and spread it out on floured dishtowels to dry.

### Cook's Tip

*The quantities given are guidelines, rather than hard-and-fast rules. Both the humidity on the day that you are making pasta and the type of flour you are using will affect the texture. The dough should not be too soft – it should be quite hard to knead – so extra flour may be required. However, too much extra will make the pasta tough and taste floury. With practice, you will get to know the "feel".*

## Shaping Pasta by Hand

Making your own noodles and pasta shapes is immensely satisfying, and not so difficult as you might expect. Who cares if the results are not perfectly uniform? Being able to shape your own tagliatelle, ravioli and tortellini is great fun. In the case of filled shapes, it means you can experiment with different fillings, and alter the size or shape. Guidance is given here for cutting or shaping three basic styles of pasta, and you will find more suggestions among the recipes in the book. Be bold – you'll be designing your own pasta in no time.

### Ravioli

**1** To make ravioli, use half the dough at a time, keeping the rest wrapped in clear film (plastic wrap). On a lightly floured surface, roll out one piece of pasta thinly to a neat rectangle. Cover with a damp, clean dishtowel and roll out an identical rectangle from the remaining pasta. Pipe or spoon small mounds of filling on to one sheet of pasta, spacing them at 4cm/1½in intervals. Brush the spaces in between with beaten egg or water.

**2** Gently lay the remaining pasta rectangle over the topped dough. Press down firmly between the pockets of filling, pushing out any air.

**3** Cut the dough into squares, using a serrated ravioli cutter or a sharp knife. Spread out the ravioli on floured dishtowels and leave to dry for about 30 minutes before cooking.

### Tortellini

**1** To make tortellini, stamp out thin rounds of pasta, using a round ravioli or biscuit (cookie) cutter. Pipe or spoon the filling into the middle then brush the edges with beaten egg or water.

**2** Fold each round into a crescent, excluding all the air. Bend the two edges round to meet each other and press them together to seal. When all the tortellini have been shaped, spread them on floured dishtowels and leave to dry for 30 minutes before cooking.

### Tagliatelle

**1** To make tagliatelle, lightly flour a thin sheet of pasta dough, then roll it up in the same way as a Swiss (jelly) roll.

**2** Cut the roll into thin slices, using a sharp knife. Immediately unravel the slices to uncurl the pasta ribbons, which should then be lightly tossed in flour and spread on floured dishtowels to dry. (To make tagliarini, cut the rolled-up dough into slices 3mm/⅛in thick. To make pappardelle, simply roll out the dough and cut it into wide ribbons.)

## Cooking Pasta

Allow 75–175g/3–6oz of pasta per person, depending on whether the pasta is for an appetizer or main course and bearing in mind the accompanying sauce.

Bring a large pan of lightly salted water to the boil. For long shapes, such as spaghetti, hold all the pasta in your hand and gradually lower it into the water until it softens sufficiently to curl round into the pan and eventually becomes immersed completely.

Sprinkle shapes into the pan, trying not to let the water go off the boil.

Cooking times vary but, on average, fresh, unfilled pasta takes 2–3 minutes, although very fine pasta may cook almost instantly. Fresh filled pasta requires 8–10 minutes. Dried unfilled pasta needs to boil for 8–12 minutes and dried filled pasta requires about 15–20 minutes. Always test by tasting – the pasta should be *al dente*; tender, but firm enough to retain a bit of "bite".

# Index

**A**

Agnolotti with taleggio & marjoram, 82
Artichokes: artichoke pasta salad, 19
  penne with, 72
Arugula see Rocket
Asparagus: asparagus & potato pasta salad with Parmesan, 18
  fried noodles with beansprouts &, 87
  garganelli with wine, cream &, 73
  somen noodles with saffron sauce, 87
  tagliatelle with mozzarella & asparagus sauce, 32
  tagliolini with, 73
Aubergines (eggplants): aubergine lasagne, 84
  pasta with caponata, 78
  pasta with coriander & grilled aubergines, 72
  pasta with tomato sauce &, 55
  penne with goat's cheese &, 40
  penne with mint pesto &, 40
  spaghetti with ricotta &, 55
Avocados: avocado & pasta salad with coriander, 17

  avocado, tomato & mozzarella pasta salad, 17
  green pasta with avocado sauce, 57

**B**

Baked tortellini with three cheeses, 46
Beancurd (tofu): fried noodles with, 68
  stir-fried beancurd with noodles, 35

Beans: three bean pasta salad, 20
Beansprouts: fried noodles with asparagus &, 87
Beetroot & ravioli soup, 11
Bolognese sauce, 65, 85
Broccoli: penne with pecans &, 49
Bucatini, 88
Bucatoni, 88
Buckwheat noodles: with cabbage, 57
  with goat's cheese, 86
Butter bean & pesto pasta, 47

**C**

Cabbage: buckwheat noodles with, 57
  pasta with Savoy cabbage & Gruyère, 60
Calabrian pasta & bean soup, 13
Campanelle, 89
Cannelloni, 90
Capelletti with tomatoes, white wine & cream, 77
Capelli, 88
Capelli d'angelo, 88
Capellini, lemon & Parmesan with herb butter, 41
Capellini with rocket & mangetouts, 27
Capellini with spinach & feta, 27
Caponata, pasta with, 78
Castiglione with Parmesan sauce, 42
Cauliflower: cauliflower soup with farfalle, 11
  pennoni rigati with, 60
Cellophane noodles, 91
  cheat's shark's fin soup, 12
  Chinese mushrooms with, 68
Cheat's Shark Fin Soup, 12
Cheese: agnolotti with taleggio & marjoram, 82
  baked tortellini with three cheeses, 46
  buckwheat noodles with goat's cheese, 86
  castiglioni with Parmesan sauce, 42
  creamy pasta with Parmesan curls, 38
  fusilli with mascarpone & spinach, 32
  home-made ravioli, 79
  lemon & Parmesan capellini

  with herb bread, 41
  macaroni & blue cheese, 43
  macaroni cheese pie, 44
  macaroni cheese with winter vegetables, 43
  macaroni soufflé, 44
  paglia e fieno with walnuts & Gorgonzola, 51
  pansotti with herbs & cheese, 82
  pasta from Pisa, 26
  penne with courgettes & goat's cheese, 42
  penne with tomatoes & mozzarella, 29
  pipe with ricotta, saffron & spinach, 51
  ravioli with cheese & herbs, 80
  Roquefort & walnut pasta salad, 20
  spaghetti with feta, 39
  stuffed conchiglie, 45
  tagliatelle with Gorgonzola sauce, 39
  tortellini with cream, butter & cheese, 46
Chickpeas: pasta soup with pulses, 13
Chinese leaves (Chinese cabbage): noodles with braised leaves, 34
Chinese mushrooms with cellophane noodles, 68
Chitarra, 88
Chitarra spaghetti with butter & herbs, 24
Conchiglie, 89
Conchiglie with tomatoes & rocket, 28
Conchiglione, 90
Cooking pasta, 93
Courgette flowers, strozzapreti with, 33
Courgettes (zucchini): pasta with courgette & walnut sauce, 49
  penne with goat's cheese &, 42

  somen noodles with, 66
Creamy tagliatelle with spinach, 63

**D**

Dough, basic pasta, 92

**E**

Egg noodles, 91
Eggplant, see Aubergine
Eliche, 89

**F**

Farfalle, 89
Farfalle with fennel & Walnut Sauce, 48
Fennel: farfalle with fennel & walnut sauce, 48
  penne with fennel concassé & blue cheese, 41
Fettuccine, 88
Fettuccine all'Alfredo, 38
Fidelini, 88
Filled pasta, 90
Fiorelli, 89
Fusilli, 89
Fusilli lunghi, 88
Fusilli with basil & parsley, 24

Fusilli with lentil & cheese sauce, 47
Fusilli with mascarpone & spinach, 32
Fusilli with tomato & balsamic vinegar, 59

**G**

Garganelli, 89
Garganelli with asparagus, wine & cream, 73
Garganelli with spring vegetables, 27
Garlic: garlic & herb pasta, 25
  spaghettini with roasted garlic, 75
Genoese minestrone, 10

**H**

Hazelnut & coriander sauce, macaroni with, 50
Heavenly tomato pasta, 56
Herbs: chitarra spaghetti with butter &, 24
    fusilli with basil & parsley, 24
    garlic & herb pasta, 25
    herb pasta, 92
    tagliatelle with fresh herbs, 25

**I**

Indian mee goreng, 86

**J**

Japanese-style noodle soup, 15

**L**

Lasagne, 90
    aubergine, 84
    baked vegetable, 83
    lasagne rolls, 85
    leek & chèvre, 83
    spinach, walnut & Gruyère, 84
Lasagnette, 90
Leek & chèvre lasagne, 83
Lemon, vermicelli with, 31
Lentils: fusilli with lentil & cheese sauce, 47
    lentil Bolognese, 85
    rustic lentil & pasta soup, 14
Linguine, 88
Linguine with rocket, 74
Linguine with sun-dried tomato pesto, 31
Long pasta, 88
Lumaconi, 90

**M**

Macaroni, 88
    macaroni & blue cheese, 43
    macaroni cheese pie, 44
    macaroni cheese with winter vegetables, 43
    macaroni soufflé, 44
    pasta with aubergine & tomato sauce, 55

vegetable & macaroni bake, 78
    with hazelnut & coriander sauce, 50
Mangetouts, capellini with rocket &, 27
Melba toast, 11
Minestrone, 10
Mushrooms: Chinese mushrooms with cellophane noodles, 68
    mushroom & chilli carbonara, 62
    mushroom Bolognese, 65
    pasta & mixed mushroom mould, 62
    rigatoni with garlic crumbs, 75
    spaghetti with black olive & mushroom sauce, 64
    spaghetti with mixed mushroom & basil sauce, 64
    tagliatelle with chanterelles, 76
    tagliatelle with mushrooms, 65
    tortellini with mushroom & cheese sauce, 76

**N**

Noodles, 91
    crispy noodles with mixed vegetables, 67
    fried noodles with beancurd, 68

fried noodles with beansprouts & asparagus, 87
    Indian mee goreng, 86
    Japanese-style noodle soup, 15
    noodle salad with sesame oil dressing, 21
    rice noodles with vegetable chilli sauce, 69
    sesame noodles with spring onions, 34
    stir-fried beancurd with, 35

teriyaki soba noodles, 35
    Thai vegetables with noodles, 34
    thamin lethok, 21
    vegetable & egg noodle ribbons, 69
    with braised leaves, 34
    see also Buckwheat noodles; Cellophane noodles; Soba noodles; Somen noodles; Vermicelli

**O**

Olives: pasta salad with, 19
    spaghetti with black olive & mushroom sauce, 64
    tagliatelle with olive & pecan sauce, 48
Orecchiette, 89
Orecchiette with tomatoes & rocket, 74

**P**

Paglia e fieno with walnuts & Gorgonzola, 51
Paglia e fieno with radicchio, 77
Pansotti with herbs & cheese, 82
Pappardelle, 88
Parpadelle tossed with grilled vegetables, 61
Pasta: basic dough, 92
    types of, 88–90
Pasta machines, 92
Pasta pie, 45
Pasta salad with olives, 19
Pasta with aubergines & tomato sauce, 55
Pasta with caponata, 78
Pasta with coriander & grilled aubergines, 72
Pasta with courgette & walnut sauce, 49
Pasta with mixed vegetable medley. 54
Pasta with nut & cream sauce, 50
Pastina, 90
Pecan nuts: tagliatelle with olive & pecan sauce, 48
Penne, 89
Penne rigati with cauliflower, 60
Penne with artichokes, 72
Penne with aubergines & goat's cheese, 40
Penne with aubergines & mint pesto, 40

Penne with broccoli & pecans, 49
Penne with courgettes & goat's cheese, 42
Penne with fennel concassé & blue cheese, 41
Penne with rocket & mozzarella, 26
Penne with tomatoes & mozzarella, 29

Peppers: chargrilled pepper salad, 16
    fusilli with onions &, 63
    spaghetti with pepper & tomato sauce, 33
Pipe, 89
Pipe rigate, 89
Pipe with ricotta, saffron & spinach, 51
Pisa, pasta from, 26
Potatoes: Sardinian ravioli, 81
    trenette with pesto, green beans &, 54
Pulses, pasta soup with, 13
Pumpkin: coriander ravioli with pumpkin filling, 80

**R**

Radicchio, paglia e fieno with, 77
Ratatouille sauce, spaghetti with, 61
Ravioli, 93
    beetroot & ravioli soup, 11
    coriander ravioli with pumpkin filling, 80
    home-made ravioli, 79
    Sardinian ravioli, 81
    with cheese & herbs, 80
Rice: thamin lethok, 21
Rice noodles, 91
Rice vermicelli see Vermicelli
Rigatoni, 89
Rigatoni with garlic crumbs, 75
Rigatoni with winter tomato sauce, 59
Rocket (arugula): capellini with mangetouts &, 27
    linguine with, 74

penne with mozzarella &, 26
Roquefort & walnut pasta salad, 20
Rotelle, 89
Ruote, 89

**S**

Sardinian ravioli, 81
Sesame noodles with spring onions, 34
Sesame oil dressing, noodle salad with, 21
Shaping pasta, 93
Shark's fin soup, cheat's, 12
Short pasta, 89
Soba noodles, 91
    teriyaki soba noodles, 35
Somen noodles, 91
    with baked cherry tomatoes, 66
    with courgettes, 66
    with saffron sauce, 87
Soufflé, macaroni, 44
Sour cream sauce, spirali with, 85
Spaghetti, 88
    chitarra spaghetti with butter & herbs, 24
    Genoese minestrone, 10
    mushroom & chilli carbonara, 62
    mushroom Bolognese, 65
    with aubergines & ricotta, 55
    with black olive & mushroom sauce, 64
    with feta, 39

    with mixed mushroom & basil sauce, 64
    with pepper & tomato sauce, 33
    with ratatouillle sauce, 61
    with sun-dried tomato sauce, 30
Spaghettini with roasted garlic, 75
Spinach: capellini with feta &, 27

creamy tagliatelle with, 63
    lasagne rolls, 85
    spinach & ricotta conchiglie, 79
    spinach pasta, 92
    spinach, walnut & Gruyère lasagne, 84
    stuffed conchiglie, 45
    thick spinach & pasta soup, 14
Spirali, 89
Spirali with sour cream sauce, 85
Spirali with tomato & cream cheese sauce, 30
Squash stuffing, tortelli with, 81
Star-gazer vegetable soup, 12
Stock, vegetable, 12
Strangozzi, 88
Strozzapreti, 89
    with courgette flowers, 33
Stuffed conchiglione, 45
Sugocasa, pasta with chilli &, 29

**T**

Tagliarini, 88
Tagliatelle, 88, 93
    double tomato tagliatelle, 28
    garlic & herb pasta, 25
    green pasta with avocado sauce, 57
    pasta with caponata, 78
    pasta with Savoy cabbage & Gruyère, 60
    sun-dried tomato & Parmesan carbonara, 56
    with chanterelles, 76
    with fresh herbs, 25
    with Gorgonzola sauce, 39
    with mozzarella & asparagus sauce, 32
    with mushrooms, 65
    with olive & pecan sauce, 48
    with spinach, 63
    with tomatoes & courgettes, 58
Tagliolini, 88
Taglioni with asparagus, 73
Teriyaki soba noodles, 35
Thai vegetables with noodles, 34
Thamin lethok, 21
Toast, Melba, 11
Tomatoes: cappelletti with white wine, cream &, 77
    conchiglie with rocket &, 28
    double tomato tagliatelle, 28
    fusilli with tomato & balsamic vinegar, 59
    heavenly tomato pasta, 56

    linguine with sun-dried tomato pesto, 31
    orecchiette with rocket &, 74
    pasta pie, 45
    pasta with sugocasa & chilli, 29
    penne with mozzarella &, 29
    rigatoni with winter tomato sauce, 59
    roasted cherry tomato & rocket salad, 16
    somen noodles with baked cherry tomatoes, 66
    spaghetti with sun-dried tomato sauce, 30
    spirali with tomato & cream cheese sauce, 30
    sun-dried tomato & Parmesan carbonara, 56
    tagliatelle with tomatoes & courgettes,58
    tomato pasta, 92
Tortelli with squash stuffing, 81
Tortellini, 93
Tortellini with cream, butter & cheese, 46
Tortellini with mushroom & cheese sauce, 76
Trenette with pesto, green beans & potatoes 54

**U**

Udon noodles, 91

**V**

Vegetables: baked vegetable lasagne, 83
    crispy noodles with mixed vegetables, 67
    garganelli with spring vegetables, 27
    noodle cakes with, 67
    pappardelle tossed with grilled vegetables, 61
    pasta with spring vegetables, 58
    pasta with mixed vegetable medley, 54

rice noodles with vegetable chilli sauce, 69
star-gazer vegetable soup, 12
Thai vegetables with noodles, 34
vegetable & egg noodle ribbons, 69
vegetable & macaroni bake, 78
vegetable & vermicelli noodle soup, 15
vegetable stock, 12
Vermicelli, 88, 91
    noodle cakes with vegetables, 67
    star-gazer vegetable soup, 12
    vegetable & vermicelli noodle soup, 15
    with lemon, 31

**W**

Walnuts: pasta with nut & cream sauce, 50
    Roquefort & walnut pasta salad, 20

Wholemeal (whole-wheat) pasta, 92
Wholewheat pasta salad, 18

**Z**

Ziti, 88
Zucchini, see courgettes